100 Days to Better English Reading Comprehension:

Intermediate-Advanced ESL Reading and Vocabulary Lessons

Jackie Bolen

www.eslspeaking.org

Table of Contents

5

About the Author: Jackie Bolen

I taught English in South Korea for 10 years to every level and type of student. I've taught every age from kindergarten kids to adults. These days, I'm teaching in Vancouver, Canada. I hold a Master of Arts in Psychology and I've completed the CELTA and DELTA certification programs

Pinterest: www.pinterest.com/eslspeaking

YouTube: www.youtube.com/c/jackiebolen

Email: jb.business.online@gmail.com

You might also be interested in these other resources (by Jackie Bolen). You can find them wherever you like to buy books:

- Advanced English Conversation Dialogues

- The Big Book of Phrasal Verbs in Use

- 100 Days to Better English Speaking (for Intermediate)

Day 1: The Last Straw

Jerry is talking to Linda about wanting to leave his wife.

Jerry: So I think I'm going to **leave my wife**.

Linda: On no! What happened? You guys always seemed like pretty **happy campers** to me.

Jerry: Well, **the last straw** was looking at my retirement accounts and seeing that most of them were **cleaned out**. Plus, we're in the red on all our other accounts too. She loves to **shop till she drops** but I didn't realize how **dire** it was until now.

Linda: Sorry to hear that. I hope you can get back **in the black**. You went **from rags to riches** once. I'm sure you can do it again.

Jerry: Hopefully, but after paying the divorce lawyers, I'll have a lot of work to **make up for lost time** on those retirement accounts. And she may also want **spousal support.**

Linda: Well, hang in there my friend. I'm here for you.

Vocabulary

the last straw: The final annoying thing before someone loses their patience. For example, a child has been misbehaving all day but his dad finally yelled at him when he wouldn't stay in his room at bedtime.

in the black: To not be in debt.

leave my wife: Separate or get a divorce.

happy campers: People that are joyful or having fun together.

cleaned out: Usually refers to money, when someone spends everything.

shop till she drops: Loves shopping and spends lots of time doing it.

dire: Very bad.

make up for lost time: Wasted time that you can't get back.

spousal support: Money paid to a former husband or wife after getting divorced.

from rags to riches: Poor to rich.

Practice

1. The food situation is now becoming _____. One of us has to go shopping!

2. Honestly, this is _____ before he gets fired.

3. We started living frugally and are now _____.

4. I want to _____. We just don't have that much in common anymore.

5. The kids were such _____ when I bought them a new trampoline.

6. My wife loves to _____ but I feel nervous about how much money she's spending.

7. I had to pay _____ after getting divorced.

8. I only started dating in my twenties. Now, I have to _____.

9. Wow! I love the story of that guy going _____ when he moved to the USA.

Answers

1. dire

2. the last straw

3. in the black

4. leave my wife

5. happy campers

6. shop till she drops

7. spousal support

8. make up for lost time

9. from rags to riches

Day 2: Black and White

Terry and Sandra are Biology classmates discussing the issue of cloning.

Terry: What did you think about the **lecture** today? Interesting, right?

Sandra: The lecture raised a lot of ethical questions for me about **cloning**. It's not a **black and white** issue. There are so many **shades of gray**.

Terry: Definitely. There should be way stricter standards for replicating living things. At the end of the day, it shouldn't only come down to the researcher's **values** and **ethics**.

Sandra: Yes, **it goes without saying**. But who will **develop** these standards? Universities? **Industry**? The government?

Terry: That **remains to be seen**. Likely it'll be a combination of those things. Cloning is still a very new thing.

Vocabulary

lecture: In a university or college, where a professor gives information by talking about it. Typically, a 2-3 hour class that is held once a week.

cloning: Making a copy of something.

black and white: There *is* a clear right and wrong.

shades of gray: There *is no* clear right and wrong.

values: Basic, fundamental beliefs about something.

ethics: Moral principles that govern a person's behavior or the conducting of an activity.

it goes without saying: It's obvious.

develop: Make something new.

industry: For-profit companies.

remains to be seen: The outcome of something is undecided at the current time.

Practice

1. That _____ was so boring. I think I fell asleep for a few minutes.

2. That company has so many issues I think because they have no core _____.

3. It's a difficult situation! There are no _____ answers here.

4. Do you think that in 100 years from now, _____ of humans will be possible?

5. The university is putting together a committee to _____ some guidelines about cloning.

6. I can't tell you what to do in this situation. It depends on your personal _____.

7. You can make more money in _____ jobs than with the government but the benefits aren't as good.

8. It _____ whether or not I'll pass that test. It was so difficult.

9. _____ that he's the best choice for an advisor but he already has so many students.

10. I enjoy studying bioethics but I don't like that are so many _____ for almost everything.

Answers

1. lecture

2. values

3. black and white

4. cloning

5. develop

6. ethics/values

7. industry

8. remains to be seen

9. it goes without saying

10. shades of gray

Day 3: The Canucks Game

There was a guy named Alex who moved to Vancouver to study English. Alex had recently moved to the city and was excited to **immerse** himself in the **local culture**. He had heard a lot about ice hockey and how passionate Canadians were about the sport. So when he found out that the Vancouver Canucks, the local hockey team, had a game coming up, Alex knew he had to experience it firsthand.

With great anticipation, Alex bought a ticket to the Canucks game at Rogers Arena. He arrived early at the arena, feeling a mix of nervousness and excitement. The atmosphere was **electric** as fans clad in blue and green jerseys filled the stadium. The sound of cheerful conversations, laughter, and the smell of freshly made popcorn filled the air.

As Alex took his seat, he noticed the giant scoreboard above the ice rink, displaying the team's logo with pride. The lights **dimmed**, and the crowd erupted in cheers as the players skated onto the ice. The game began, and the speed and skill of the players amazed Alex. He could feel the intensity of the game, and it was infectious.

Throughout the game, Alex couldn't help but join in the chants and cheers with the other fans. He learned the popular chants like "Go Canucks, Go!" and "Let's go, Vancouver!" It didn't matter if he didn't understand every word; the energy in the arena carried him along.

During the intermission, Alex decided to explore the concourse. They discovered various food stands offering classic Canadian treats like poutine and maple syrup-flavored donuts. Alex indulged in a delicious hot dog, feeling grateful for this wonderful cultural experience. Of course, he bought a couple of very expensive beers as well.

As the game continued, the Canucks scored a goal, and the crowd erupted in an explosion of joy. The unity felt in that moment was incredible. Alex found himself high-fiving strangers, connected by his shared love for the team.

Even though the Canucks didn't win that particular game, Alex left the arena with a **newfound** appreciation for ice hockey and the Vancouver Canucks. He felt a sense of belonging and understood why hockey was such an **integral** part of Canadian culture.

Walking back home, Alex couldn't help but **reflect** on the amazing experience he had just had. He realized that attending a Vancouver Canucks game was more than just watching a sport; it was about being part of a community, celebrating together, and embracing **the spirit of the game**.

From that day forward, Alex continued to support the Canucks, attending games whenever possible. He made new friends, bonded over shared victories and defeats, and became a true fan of the team. The Vancouver Canucks had not only given Alex a memorable evening but also a lifelong passion for ice hockey and a deep love for his new home.

Vocabulary

immerse: Involve oneself deeply in something.

local culture: The way of life in a certain location.

electric: Exciting; thrilling.

dimmed: Became less bright.

newfound: Recently discovered.

integral: Very important; key.

reflect: Think back upon something.

the spirit of the game: Sportsmanship; fair play, playing for the love of the game.

Comprehension Questions

1. Did Alex know a lot about hockey before moving to Vancouver?
2. What was the atmosphere like at the arena?
3. What are some examples of unity amongst the fans?
4. Do you think Alex will be a Canucks fan for life?
5. Do Canadians love hockey?

Answers

1. No, he didn't.

2. It was very exciting—lots of sights, smells, sounds, and Canucks fans.

3. They were united in their chants and cheers, as well as when the Canucks scored a goal.

4. Yes, most likely! He watched games after that whenever possible.

5. Yes, Canadians are very passionate about hockey.

Let's Talk More

1. Have you ever been to a professional hockey game? What was that experience like? If you haven't, you can talk about an experience at another sport.

2. Do you think that sport can positively unite countries?

3. Do professional athletes get paid too much money in your opinion?

4. If you have/had children, would you ever encourage them to try to become professional athletes?

5. Do you think sports like hockey or American football are too violent?

Day 4: Tennis Match

Sid is talking about his tennis injury.

Kay: So what did you get up to **this weekend** Sid? Wait...what happened to your face? That looks like it hurts.

Sid: I had a **tennis match** and I got hit in the face with the ball. It's just a **minor injury** but I had to go to the **emergency room** to **get stitches**.

Kay: Good thing you didn't sustain **serious injuries**. It could have been bad if you'd gotten hit in the eye.

Sid: Yeah, nothing serious as long as I **take antibiotics** to **prevent infection**. The worst thing was that we lost the match because I had to leave to go to the hospital.

Kay: I can't believe that you're worried about that!

Vocabulary

this weekend: Previous, or next Saturday or Sunday (depends on when talking about it— earlier, or later in the week).

tennis match: Tennis game that consists of 3 or 5 sets.

minor injury: Not a serious injury.

emergency room: Place to get immediate medical treatment.

get stitches: Using a needle and thread to close a cut in the skin.

serious injuries: A big medical problem.

take antibiotics: Taking pills to stop the spread of infection.

prevent infection: Taking antibiotics or cleaning a wound so that bacteria don't get out of control.

14

Practice

1. Do you want to catch a movie with me _____?

2. Clean the wound first to help _____.

3. Did you have to _____ for that cut?

4. It looks worse than it is. It's just a _____.

5. Did you see the _____ between Nadal and Federer?

6. You'll have to _____ for that but please finish them all.

7. Please call 911 for _____.

8. I think I need to go to the _____. My arm is probably broken.

Answers

1. this weekend

2. prevent infection

3. get stitches

4. minor injury

5. tennis match

6. take antibiotics

7. serious injuries

8. emergency room

Day 5: The Clever Woodcutter

In a small village **nestled** between hills and forests, there lived a **woodcutter** named Jack. Jack was known throughout the village for his hard work and honesty. One day, he faced a **dilemma** that would test his cleverness.

One winter morning, as Jack entered the forest to gather firewood, he noticed a large tree. Its branches were covered with thick snow, and Jack marveled at it. He decided to chop it down for firewood, but as he swung his axe, something unexpected happened.

The tree, being magical, spoke to Jack. "Dear woodcutter, I am the oldest tree in this forest. **Spare** me, and I will grant you three wishes." Jack, surprised and intrigued, agreed to spare the tree's life. The wise woodcutter thought carefully about his wishes. Instead of asking for wealth or grandeur, Jack chose wisely.

For his first wish, Jack asked for a small, cozy cottage. In an instant, a charming cottage appeared on the edge of the forest. Jack was delighted.

For his second wish, Jack asked for a pouch that would never run out of gold coins. The magical pouch appeared, and every time he reached inside, it was filled with gold. Jack was content but still had one wish left.

For his final wish, Jack thought of the well-being of his village. He asked for the health and prosperity of his fellow villagers. The ancient tree granted his wish, and from that day forward, the village flourished.

Word of Jack's cleverness and kindness spread far and wide. People from neighboring villages came to seek his advice, and Jack became known as the wisest woodcutter in the land.

The Moral

The moral of the story is that true wisdom lies in making choices that benefit not only oneself but also the community. Jack's clever decisions brought prosperity to his village, showing that kindness and selflessness are the keys to a fulfilling life.

Vocabulary

woodcutter: A person who cuts wood.

spare: Save; not use.

nestled: Partially hidden.

dilemma: A problem.

Comprehension Questions

1. What made Jack a wise woodcutter?
2. What did Jack find in the forest one winter day?
3. What did the magical tree offer Jack in exchange for sparing its life?
4. What were Jack's three wishes?
5. How did Jack's choices affect the village?

Answers

1. Jack was considered wise because he made clever choices that not only benefited himself but also brought happiness to his village.
2. Jack found a special, magical tree in the forest.
3. The magical tree offered Jack three wishes in exchange for sparing its life.
4. Jack's first wish was for a cozy cottage, the second wish was for a pouch that never ran out of gold coins, and the third wish was for the health and happiness of his village.
5. Jack's choices brought prosperity and happiness to the village. The health and well-being of the villagers improved, and the village thrived.

Day 6: Weather Forecast

Ted and Lindsay are looking at the weather forecast and making plans for the weekend.

Ted: What's the **weather forecast** looking like this weekend? We should get out for a hike.

Lindsay: Let me check. Clear skies on Saturday but **scattered showers** on Sunday. **Hot and humid** both days.

Ted: If we're going to go to Mount Hood, we need to be **prepared for anything**. It can go from calm to **gale-force winds on a dime**.

Lindsay: That happened last time I was there. Just **light rain** at first and then the **storm clouds** rolled in and there were **wind gusts** of more than 100 km/h. It was wild.

Vocabulary

weather forecast: Prediction of future weather.

let me check: Give me a minute to find the answer to something.

clear skies: Not cloudy.

scattered showers: Rain that is on and off.

hot and humid: Muggy.

prepared for anything: Ready to face any situation.

gale-force winds: Very strong wind.

on a dime: Suddenly.

light rain: Not raining heavily.

storm clouds: Clouds that may produce rain, snow, hail, thunder, etc.

wind gusts: Bursts of wind after periods of relative calm.

Practice

1. There will be _____ of more than 150 km/hour today.

2. _____ at night usually means good weather the next day.

3. His personality changes _____.

4. It's so _____. I just want to sit next to a pool.

5. You have to be _____ with this job.

6. I'm not sure if we have that in stock. _____.

7. There are some serious _____ over there. I think we should turn around.

8. The forecast showed some _____. Don't forget your umbrella.

9. What's the _____ for Japan this week? I need to know how to pack for my trip.

10. I know it doesn't seem like it, but _____ are not ideal when sailing.

Answers

1. wind gusts

2. clear skies

3. on a dime

4. hot and humid

5. prepared for anything

6. let me check

7. storm clouds

8. scattered showers/light rain

9. weather forecast

10. gale-force winds

Day 7: The Bear and the Bee

In a vast and vibrant meadow, there resided a **formidable** bear and a **diligent** bee. The bear, with his thick fur and powerful stature, often roamed the meadow, while the bee, small yet tirelessly energetic, buzzed from flower to flower.

One sunny afternoon, as the bee was busy collecting nectar to create golden honey, the bear, enticed by the sweet aroma, approached with curiosity. "Greetings, dear bee," said the bear. "Your honey looks delectable. Might I have a taste?"

Understanding the bear's appetite, the clever bee proposed a friendly **contest**. "Certainly, Mr. Bear," replied the bee. "Let's see who can gather the most flowers. The winner shall enjoy the honey!"

Excited by the competition, the bear agreed, and they set off to collect flowers. The bee darted swiftly among the blossoms, while the bear, using his massive paws, **lumbered** around and carefully selected vibrant flowers.

As the sun dipped below the horizon, they tallied their collections. To the bear's surprise, the bee had gathered more flowers. The bee grinned and remarked, "You see, Mr. Bear, hard work and diligence triumph over size."

Impressed by the lesson, the bear nodded appreciatively. "You are right, industrious bee. I've learned that the effort we put in is often more important than our size and strength. Thank you for this valuable lesson."

From that day forward, the bear and the bee became steadfast friends. They shared not only the honey but also the beauty of the meadow, appreciating the different strengths each brought to their friendship. And so, in the vibrant meadow, the bear and the bee continued to live harmoniously, savoring the sweet rewards of cooperation and hard work.

The Moral

The moral of the story is that working hard is important. Even if someone is big and strong, someone smaller who works really hard can achieve success too. In the story, the bee showed the bear that effort matters more than size.

Vocabulary

contest: An event where people compete with each other.

lumbered: Moved slowly and awkwardly.

formidable: Large and powerful.

diligent: Showing care about what one is doing.

Comprehension Questions

1. Why did the bear approach the bee in the first place?
2. What challenge did the bee propose to the bear?
3. Who won the flower-gathering challenge, and how did they determine the winner?
4. What did the bear learn from the bee's challenge?
5. How did the bear and the bee's relationship change after the challenge?

Answers

1. The bear approached the bee because he wanted to taste the delicious honey the bee was making.
2. The bee challenged the bear to see who could gather the most flowers, and the winner would get to enjoy the honey.
3. The bee won the challenge by gathering more flowers. They counted the flowers to determine the winner.
4. The bear learned that hard work and effort are more important than size and strength.
5. The bear and the bee became friends, sharing not only the honey but also enjoying the beauty of the meadow together.

Day 8: In a Nutshell

A TA is talking about an issue that he wants his students to discuss in an Ethics class.

Here's the situation that I want you to discuss in small groups. A large **manufacturer** of infant formula had two recipes. One of them, containing all the recommended vitamins and minerals is for sale in countries like the USA, Canada, and Australia. The other one, which is cheaper to make, doesn't contain the **optimal** nutritional balance but instead has some **fillers** in it. It is an **inferior** product in almost all ways and is sold in countries with fewer governmental **regulations** about this kind of thing. It doesn't kill the babies but they don't get **adequate** nutrition to **thrive**.

I want you to talk about who's to **blame**. Is it the government in those poorer countries for not having better regulations and **oversight**? Or, is the company negligent and should be **punished** for selling an inferior product? Or, are the parents somehow at fault? The parents are desperate for someone to answer for this and the company narrowly avoided bankruptcy once the scandal became public knowledge.

Vocabulary

manufacturer: A company that makes things.

optimal: Ideal.

fillers: Something cheap that is added to something to make it less expensive to make.

inferior: Not as good.

regulations: Rules or laws about something.

adequate: Acceptable; good enough.

thrive: Do well.

blame: Responsibility for something that went wrong.

oversight: Inspections for quality control purposes.

punished: Consequences for doing something against the law or unethical practices.

Practice

1. There are only a few _____ left in my town.

2. His meals don't have _____ nutrition in them. I'm worried he'll get sick.

3. That company should get _____ for selling such a terrible product.

4. He seems to _____ with a heavier workload. It's impressive.

5. It's cheaper but it's an _____ product. You won't be happy with it.

6. This hamburger doesn't taste good. I think it has lots of _____ in it.

7. Who's to _____ here? Tom and Jerry were working on that project together.

8. The government should have more _____ about medical testing on humans.

9. It sounds like that department needs some more _____. They keep making mistakes.

10. The _____ balance for most meals is equal parts fat, carbs, and protein.

Answers

1. manufacturers

2. adequate

3. punished

4. thrive

5. inferior

6. fillers

7. blame

8. regulations

9. oversight

10. optimal

Day 9: Christmas in May

Sam was hanging out with his friend Carrie in Burnaby, a suburb of Vancouver. They were at Deer Lake, a popular park. Sam and Carrie were walking around the lake, enjoying a beautiful spring day, when they saw **a bunch** of trucks, equipment, and people. It was quite unusual to see something like that at a public park. "I wonder what this is?" said Sam. "I'm not sure, let's take a closer look," replied Carrie.

So they went to check it out but were soon stopped by a person with a **walkie-talkie**. "You can't come into this area," said the person. Sam and Carrie asked that person what was going on. The person said that they were filming a movie. There are lots of TV shows and movies filmed in Vancouver, so it wasn't so unusual to see this. They asked the person which movie they were filming, and she said that it was a "**made for TV movie**." She also mentioned that it wasn't something they would have heard of.

Sam was still curious about it and wondered if anyone famous was in the movie that he might recognize. He suggested walking around the fence that blocked off access to the set to see if they could get a better look. They walked for a minute or two and then started to see an unusual scene—lots of snow, Christmas lights and other Christmas decorations. The set was a small town designed to look like it was winter, even though May is springtime in Canada. It looked realistic, and they were impressed at how well done it was.

They **peered** through the fence, trying to catch **a glimpse** of the **stars**. But, they could only see lots of cables, crew members, cameras, makeup artists, hair stylists, a snack table and things like that. They couldn't see any actors or actresses. It looked like everyone was setting up because they didn't hear a director yelling things like action or cut. They took a few pictures and continued their walk. It was an interesting experience for them, but they were a little bit disappointed not to see any famous people.

Vocabulary

a bunch = Many; a lot of.

walkie-talkies: Radios that people use to talk to each other.

made for TV movie: A movie that never plays in movie theaters. Instead, it goes directly to TV or online streaming websites.

peered: Looked closely.

a **glimpse:** A brief look at something.

stars: In this situation, refers to actors or actresses.

Comprehension Questions

1. What season is it in May in Canada?

2. Was the snow that they saw real?

3. Did the Christmas scene look real?

4. Did Sam and Carrie see any actors or actresses?

5. Could they go onto the set?

6. What were they disappointed about?

Answers

1. It's spring.

2. No, the snow was fake.

3. Yes, it looked quite realistic.

4. No, they didn't.

5. No, they couldn't. They had to look at it through a fence.

6. They hoped to see some stars.

Let's Talk More

1. Have you ever seen a TV or movie show being made? What did you think?

2. Have you ever met anyone famous? If not, would you like to?

3. Are there any TV shows or movies filmed in your city? Where are they usually filmed?

4. Do you spend a lot of time watching TV shows and movies?

5. How would you feel if a movie was being filmed in your neighborhood? Would you be excited, or annoyed by it?

Day 10: Exploring the Depths of the Human Mind

Understanding the complexities of human behavior and the intricate workings of the mind is the fundamental pursuit of psychology. As an academic discipline, psychology seeks to unravel the mysteries of thought, emotion, and behavior, providing valuable insights into the essence of what it means to be human. This introductory exploration into psychology serves as a gateway to a diverse and dynamic field that encompasses a **myriad** of perspectives, theories, and methodologies.

The Definition and Scope of Psychology

Psychology, derived from the Greek words "psyche" (meaning soul or mind) and "logos" (meaning study), is commonly defined as the scientific study of behavior and mental processes. This broad definition underscores the comprehensive nature of the discipline, which extends its reach from the observable actions of individuals to the **intricate** processes occurring within the mind.

The scope of psychology is vast, encompassing a wide array of subfields such as clinical psychology, cognitive psychology, developmental psychology, social psychology, and more. Each subfield focuses on specific aspects of human behavior and cognition, contributing to the richness and diversity of psychological knowledge.

Historical Foundations

To comprehend the evolution of psychology, it is essential to **delve** into its historical foundations. Psychology's roots can be traced back to ancient civilizations, where philosophers pondered questions related to the mind and behavior. However, it was in the late 19th century that psychology emerged as a formal discipline with the establishment of Wilhelm Wundt's experimental psychology laboratory in Leipzig, Germany, in 1879. Wundt's emphasis on the scientific study of **consciousness** laid the groundwork for the systematic exploration of psychological phenomena.

The subsequent decades witnessed the development of various schools of thought, each offering unique perspectives on the mind and behavior. From Sigmund Freud's psychoanalytic theory, which delved into the unconscious mind, to John B. Watson's behaviorism, which focused on observable behaviors, the early years of psychology were marked by a diversity of **theoretical** approaches.

Modern Perspectives

Contemporary psychology has evolved into a multifaceted discipline, embracing a range of perspectives that reflect the complexity of human nature. The psychodynamic perspective, influenced by Freud's work, continues to explore the unconscious mind and the impact of early experiences on behavior. The behavioral perspective emphasizes the role of observable behaviors and environmental influences in shaping individuals.

Cognitive psychology, on the other hand, investigates mental processes such as memory, perception, and problem-solving. Humanistic psychology emphasizes personal growth, self-actualization, and the pursuit of one's potential. The social-cultural perspective examines the influence of cultural and social factors on behavior, recognizing the interconnectedness of individuals within their societal contexts.

Research Methods in Psychology

The scientific nature of psychology is manifested through rigorous research methods employed to investigate hypotheses and validate theories. Researchers utilize various approaches, including experiments, surveys, case studies, and observational studies, each tailored to address specific research questions. The scientific method is a cornerstone of psychological inquiry, promoting systematic observation, data collection, analysis, and interpretation.

The Application of Psychological Knowledge

Psychology is not only an academic pursuit but also a discipline with real-world applications. Clinical psychologists apply their understanding of mental health to diagnose and treat psychological disorders, while counseling psychologists assist individuals in coping with life's challenges. Industrial-organizational psychologists contribute to workplace efficiency and employee well-being, and forensic psychologists apply their expertise to legal and criminal justice settings.

The Role of Nature and Nurture

A central debate within psychology revolves around the relative contributions of nature and nurture to human development. The nature-nurture debate explores the interplay between genetic factors (nature) and environmental influences (nurture) in shaping individual differences. Contemporary perspectives recognize the intricate interaction between genetics and environment, highlighting the dynamic and reciprocal nature of developmental processes.

Conclusion

In conclusion, this introduction merely scratches the surface of the vast and dynamic field of psychology. From its historical roots to the contemporary perspectives and diverse applications, psychology offers a captivating journey into the intricacies of the human mind. As we embark on this exploration, we invite you to delve deeper into the rich tapestry of psychological knowledge, where the quest to understand the complexities of human behavior unfolds with every discovery and inquiry. Through the lens of psychology, we gain valuable insights that not only inform our academic endeavors but also enhance our understanding of ourselves and the world around us.

Vocabulary

discipline: A field of study or branch of knowledge, in this context, referring to the systematic study of human behavior and mental processes.

perspectives: Different viewpoints or approaches used to understand and interpret psychological phenomena, such as the psychodynamic, behavioral, cognitive, humanistic, and social-cultural perspectives mentioned in the passage.

methodologies: The systematic procedures or techniques employed in research, including experiments, surveys, case studies, and observational studies, to gather and analyze data in psychology.

foundations: The fundamental principles or origins upon which a particular field, in this case, psychology, is built and developed, encompassing historical roots and foundational theories.

cognition: The mental processes involved in acquiring, processing, storing, and using information, a key focus of cognitive psychology mentioned in the passage.

psychoanalytic theory: A psychological perspective, pioneered by Sigmund Freud, that emphasizes the role of the unconscious mind, childhood experiences, and the interplay of conscious and unconscious forces in shaping behavior.

behaviorism: A school of thought in psychology, associated with John B. Watson, that focuses on the study of observable behaviors and the influence of environmental factors on behavior.

humanistic psychology: A psychological perspective that emphasizes individual potential, personal growth, and the pursuit of self-actualization as essential aspects of human experience.

nature-nurture debate: A longstanding discussion within psychology exploring the relative contributions of genetic factors (nature) and environmental influences (nurture) to human development and behavior.

scientific method: A systematic approach to research characterized by observation, hypothesis formulation, experimentation, data collection, analysis, and interpretation, used in psychology to study and understand various phenomena.

Vocabulary Challenge

1. Myriad, in the first paragraph is closest in meaning to:

    a) a variety

    b) a very large number

    c) a few

    d) a number of

2. Intricate, in the second paragraph is closest in meaning to:

    a) simple

    b) unknowable

    c) complicated

    d) mysterious

3. Delve, in the fourth paragraph is closest in meaning to:

    a) excavate

    b) learn a bit about something

    c) go

    d) thoroughly research

4. Consciousness, in the fourth paragraph is closest in meaning to:

    a) action

    b) reason

    c) awareness

    d) morality

5. Theoretical, in the fifth paragraph is closest in meaning to:

    a) based on ideas

    b) based on experience

    c) based on observation

    d) practical

Answers

1. b
2. c
3. d
4. c
5. a

Multiple Choice Questions

1. What is the definition of psychology?

   a) The study of ancient civilizations

   b) The exploration of conscious experiences

   c) The examination of environmental influences

   d) The scientific study of behavior and mental processes

2. Who established the first experimental psychology laboratory in Leipzig in 1879?

   a) John B. Watson

   b) Wilhelm Wundt

   c) Sigmund Freud

   d) B.F. Skinner

3. Which psychological perspective emphasizes the unconscious mind and the impact of early experiences on behavior?

   a) Cognitive psychology

   b) Humanistic psychology

   c) Psychoanalytic theory

   d) Behaviorism

4. What is a cornerstone of psychological inquiry that involves systematic observation, data collection, analysis, and interpretation?

    a) Philosophical method

    b) Experimental design

    c) Scientific method

    d) Observational approach

5. Which perspective in psychology focuses on observable behaviors and environmental influences?

    a) Psychodynamic perspective

    b) Behavioral perspective

    c) Cognitive perspective

    d) Humanistic perspective

6. Which term refers to the interplay between genetic factors and environmental influences in shaping individual differences?

    a) Nature-versus-nurture argument

    b) Genetic determinism

    c) Environmental determinism

    d) Nature-nurture debate

7. What is the central debate in psychology regarding human development and behavior?

    a) Nature-nurture debate

    b) Historical foundations

    c) Scientific methodologies

    d) Perspectives in psychology

8. Which subfield of psychology is concerned with workplace efficiency and employee well-being?

   a) Clinical psychology

   b) Counseling psychology

   c) Industrial-organizational psychology

   d) Forensic psychology

9. What term encompasses the fundamental principles or origins upon which psychology is built and developed?

   a) Philosophical roots

   b) Historical foundations

   c) Scientific perspectives

   d) Methodological principles

10. Which psychological perspective investigates mental processes such as memory, perception, and problem-solving?

   a) Social-cultural perspective

   b) Cognitive psychology

   c) Behaviorism

   d) Humanistic psychology

Answers

1. d
2. b
3. c
4. c
5. b
6. d
7. a
8. c
9. b
10. b

Day 11: Bitter Divorce

Sierra and Brian are talking about their friends getting divorced.

Sierra: Did you **hear the news**? Jeremy and Katie are going through a **bitter divorce**.

Brian: Really? What about the kids? Are they doing **joint custody** or **sole custody**?

Sierra: Joint custody. Jeremy will have them **on weekends** but he has to **pay child support**.

Brian: Poor kids. That was a pretty **dysfunctional family** and they've already had a **troubled childhood**.

Sierra: A **broken home** might be better than all that conflict though. It's too bad that Jeremy and Katie aren't **on good terms**.

Vocabulary

hear the news: Catch the latest gossip.

bitter divorce: A divorce that is hostile with both people feeling angry towards the other.

joint custody: When divorced parents each spend some time taking care of their children.

sole custody: When a divorced parent is responsible 100% of the time for the children.

on weekends: On Saturday and Sunday.

pay child support: When one divorced parent has to give money to the other parent to help pay for the care of the children.

dysfunctional family: A family with many problems.

troubled childhood: Growing up in a family or situation with a lot of problems.

broken home: A home where the parents are divorced.

on good terms: Friendly and get along well.

Practice

1. Thankfully my former boss and I are _____. I need him for a reference.

2. I grew up in a _____ but have worked hard to overcome this.

3. Alex and Jen seem to be doing well with their _____ agreement.

4. Did you _____ ? Jeremy cheated on his wife.

5. _____, I like to spend as much time outside as possible.

6. He's had a _____ so far. I'm surprised that he still does well at school.

7. I want to get _____ of the kids. Tom is a terrible father.

8. I grew up in a _____ and have tried my best to make things better for my kids.

9. I had such a _____ but I'm happy that I don't have to see him anymore.

10. She does _____ but it should be way more than $500 a month I think.

Answers

1. on good terms

2. broken home

3. joint custody

4. hear the news

5. on weekends

6. troubled childhood

7. sole custody

8. dysfunctional family

9. bitter divorce

10. pay child support

Day 12: Who is That?

Jay was at the movie theater with his two friends, Keith and Tony. They were going to watch the new Superman movie. It was popular and difficult to get tickets to. But his friend Keith **reserved** some online for them. He was good at doing stuff like that.

They had to wait in line at the theater to **pick up** their tickets. It was a Friday night, so it was quite busy. Just in front of them was a group of women around the same age as them. Jay noticed one of the women in front of him. She had long, beautiful hair and was wearing nice jeans and a sweater. "Who is that?," he thought to himself, "She is beautiful."

Jay was **lost in his own thoughts** about the woman in front of him and not listening to his friends. Keith and Tony laughed loudly at a joke, and the woman turned around to see who was laughing. She looked at all of them and then smiled at Jay. They made **eye contact,** and he smiled back. Jay wanted to talk to her, but he was nervous so he didn't.

They finally got their tickets and went to the **concession** to get some drinks and popcorn for the movie. Jay told his friends about this beautiful woman. They said that he should go say hi, but he knew that he never would! He was too **shy** to do that kind of thing. His friends said he was making a mistake and that he'd regret it.

They got their popcorn and drinks, and Tony grabbed a napkin. He asked someone who worked at the movie theater for a pen. Jay thought it was strange to be asking for a pen at the movie theater but didn't pay attention to him. Tony asked Jay to show him which woman he thought was beautiful. He pointed her out, sitting on a bench, waiting for the movie to start. Tony walked over and handed her the napkin.

Jay said, "TONY! What did you do?" Tony said, "I wrote down your name and phone number on the napkin and said that you wanted to go on a date with her. You're welcome! Hahahaha!"

Then, they had to go into the movie theater. They sat down, and Jay's phone **buzzed**. It was the woman, introducing herself. She said that they should go for a drink after the movie. Jay quickly said yes, and they made plans to meet at a pub that was very close to the movie theater. Jay was excited and could hardly concentrate on the movie! It seemed to go on forever.

Vocabulary

reserved: Booked ahead of time. For example, tickets or a table at a restaurant.

pick up: Get something or someone from somewhere.

lost in his own thoughts: Thinking about something, not paying attention to other people; daydreaming.

eye contact: When two people look directly into each other's eyes.

concession: A place to buy snacks or drinks at a movie theater or sports event.

shy: Finds it difficult to talk to people, especially people they don't know well.

buzzed: Made a sound or vibration, usually refers to a cellphone when you get a message.

Comprehension Questions

1. Who got the tickets for them?
2. Who noticed the beautiful woman?
3. When did Jay first notice her?
4. How did Jay get her phone number?
5. Is Jay going to meet the woman?
6. Do you think that Tony is a good friend? Why?

Answers

1. Keith reserved the tickets.
2. Jay noticed the woman.
3. He noticed her when they were standing in line at the movie theater.
4. Tony gave Jay's phone number to the woman on a napkin.
5. Yes, Jay is going to meet the woman after the movie.
6. (many answers possible).

Let's Talk More

1. Would you ever do something similar to what Tony did?

2. How would you react if someone approached you like that in a public place?

3. Have you met a boyfriend or girlfriend on a dating app? How about "in real life?"

4. What are some movie theater etiquette rules (how to be polite) in your country?

5. Do you prefer to watch movies at home or in a movie theater? Why?

Day 13: Emotional Wreck

Nathan is telling Jeremy about his weekend.

Jeremy: Hey, how was your weekend?

Nathan: It started well. I **went swimming** with the kids and **did yoga**. But, Tim **broke his leg** at his **soccer game**. He has a **vivid imagination** so I didn't believe him at first but we **went to the hospital** and there was a big break. I'm an **emotional wreck** right now.

Jeremy: Oh, that sounds like tough times. I hope he's okay.

Nathan: He'll recover but he has to have a cast on for at least six weeks. What did you get up to?

Jeremy: I **played tennis** and had a **first date** with someone I **met online.** It went well and we're going to see each other next weekend.

Vocabulary

went swimming: Swam.

did yoga: Did a yoga workout.

broke his leg: Broke a bone in his leg.

soccer game: A soccer match.

vivid imagination: Active imagination.

emotional wreck: In a bad state; anxious, worried, depressed, etc.

played tennis: Had a tennis game or practice.

first date: Spending time together with a romantic interest for the first time.

met online: Meeting a romantic partner on a dating app like *Tinder* as opposed to in real life.

Practice

1. My husband and I _____.

2. My daughter has a _____.

3. I _____ this morning and now I feel great. I'm so relaxed!

4. I had a _____ with someone last night and I think we're going to meet up again.

5. I _____ with my kids but it was frustrating because they couldn't hit the ball well.

6. I _____ this morning very early. I got there when the pool opened at 6:00.

7. Will you come to watch my _____ this weekend?

8. I was an _____ when my grandmother died.

9. My husband _____ at work last week and will be off for at least three months.

Answers

1. met online

2. vivid imagination

3. did yoga

4. first date

5. played tennis

6. went swimming

7. soccer game

8. emotional wreck

9. broke his leg

Day 14: Compare and Contrast

Lindsey and Sam are talking about an assignment.

Lindsey: So what do we have to do? I didn't understand. **Compare** and **contrast** Sweden and Canada's responses to Covid-19?

Sam: Yes, exactly. We have to give a **summary** of the **response** of each country, along with a **timeline**. Essentially, **trace** the spread of the virus. Then comment on any **fundamental flaws** or **errors** that they made trying to reduce the number of deaths.

Lindsey: Okay, I see. So I guess the **desired outcome** is the same for each country—to **minimize** the number of deaths. They just went about it differently.

Sam: Yes, I've started doing some research. It's quite interesting to see the differing actions and resulting **statistics**.

Vocabulary

compare: Look for the similarities in two or more things.

contrast: Look for the differences in two or more things.

summary: Brief overview.

response: Action taken as a result of something that happened.

timeline: Arranging events by time from the beginning to end.

trace: Find or uncover a source or course of something after some investigation.

fundamental flaws: Underlying problems in the basic design or substance of a thing.

errors: Mistakes

desired outcome: Best possible result.

minimize: Make smaller or lesser.

Practice

1. Please _____ the findings from these two papers.

2. There are so many _____ with this project. Nothing we do now can fix it.

3.   Please try to _____ your mistakes in the lab or you won't get accurate results.

4. I didn't read the entire thing—just the _____.

5. Can you _____ Covid-19 infections using social media posts?

6. The _____ between rainfall in Vancouver and Riyadh is striking.

7. The _____ is that everyone will pass this class but that's mostly up to you.

8. What's the _____ here? I need to understand who did what first.

9. Why is this returning so many _____? We've done something wrong.

10. Trudeau's _____ to Covid-19 was okay but not what I would have done.

Answers

1. compare

2. fundamental flaws

3. minimize

4. summary

5. trace

6. contrast

7. desired outcome

8. timeline

9. errors

10. response

Day 15: The Boy Who Cried Wolf

Once upon a time, in a small village, there lived a young boy named Sam. Sam was responsible for watching over the village's flock of sheep. One day, feeling a bit mischievous, Sam thought it would be amusing to play a **trick** on the **villagers**.

He climbed to the top of a hill and shouted, "Wolf! Wolf! A big, scary wolf is coming to get our sheep!"

Hearing the boy's cry, the villagers hurriedly grabbed their tools and ran to the hill to help. However, when they reached the top, they found no wolf. Sam couldn't stop laughing at the villagers' puzzled faces.

The next day, Sam decided to play the same prank again. Once more, he cried, "Wolf! Wolf! A **fierce** wolf is **attacking** our sheep!"

Concerned for their flock, the villagers rushed to the hill, only to discover Sam's trick once again. This time, they were not amused, and they scolded Sam for his dishonesty.

A few days later, a real wolf appeared on the outskirts of the village. The frightened sheep bleated loudly, and Sam, genuinely scared this time, screamed, "Wolf! Wolf! A dangerous wolf is here!"

However, the villagers, remembering Sam's previous false alarms, hesitated to believe him. They thought he was playing another trick and chose not to respond. Sadly, the wolf attacked the flock, and some sheep were lost.

Sam realized the consequences of his actions. The villagers, disappointed and saddened, explained the importance of **honesty** and trust. From that day forward, Sam learned that telling the truth was crucial, and he worked hard to regain the villagers' trust. The fable of the boy who cried wolf taught everyone in the village the importance of being truthful, as **credibility** is earned through honest words and actions.

The Moral

The moral of the story is that it's important to tell the truth. If we don't tell the truth, people might not believe us when we need help. Being honest is the right thing to do.

Vocabulary

trick: Deceive or outwit.

villagers: People who live in a village (small town).

attacking: Taking aggressive action.

honesty: The quality of telling the truth.

fierce: intense; aggressive.

credibility: The quality of being trusted and believed.

Comprehension Questions

1. Why did Sam shout "Wolf! Wolf!" the first time?
2. How did the villagers respond to Sam's first and second cries for help?
3. What happened when a real wolf came to the village?
4. What did Sam learn from the villagers' reaction to his pranks?
5. What is the moral of the story?

Answers

1. Sam shouted as a prank to trick the villagers and see their reaction.
2. The villagers rushed to help when Sam shouted about the wolf, but they were disappointed when they found out it was a trick the second time.
3. When a real wolf came, Sam shouted for help, but the villagers didn't believe him because of his earlier false alarms. The wolf attacked the sheep.
4. Sam learned that being honest is important because the villagers didn't believe him when a real wolf came.
5. The moral of the story is that it's crucial to tell the truth because if we lie, people may not trust us when we really need help.

Day 16: The Development of Grammar

Language, as the **bedrock** of human communication, has undergone a fascinating evolution, with grammar serving as a crucial element in its development.

Early Foundations of Grammar: Innate Understanding

At the **dawn** of language, humans exhibited an innate capacity for grammar. From the babbling stages of infancy to the formation of basic sentence structures, early linguistic development showcased an inherent grasp of grammatical principles.

Emergence of Written Language: Shaping Structure and Clarity

The introduction of written language marked a significant milestone, bringing forth rules and conventions to maintain **clarity**. Ancient civilizations like the Sumerians and Egyptians developed scripts, influencing the structuring of grammatical rules.

Latin Influence in the Middle Ages: Prescriptive Norms

During the Middle Ages, Latin became the language of scholars and **elites**. Prescriptive grammar manuals emphasized "correct" language usage, shaping grammatical **norms** in various European languages and establishing a foundation for linguistic standards.

Renaissance and Modern Grammar: Vernacular Languages Resurge

The Renaissance witnessed a shift from Latin to vernacular languages. This period saw a renewed interest in vernacular grammatical structures, with influential figures like William Lily contributing to the codification of English grammar. The printing press facilitated widespread access to grammatical knowledge.

Enlightenment and Descriptive Grammar: Language in Action

The Enlightenment era departed from prescriptive grammar, adopting a more descriptive approach. Scholars like Sir William Temple and John Locke observed language in action, giving rise to descriptive grammar that aimed to describe language based on how it was naturally spoken and written.

Scientific Inquiry in the 19th Century: Linguistics as a Discipline

The 19th century witnessed the formalization of linguistics as a discipline. Scholars like Ferdinand de Saussure and Wilhelm von Humboldt explored the deep structures of language, contributing valuable insights to our understanding of grammar.

Generative Grammar in the 20th Century: Cognitive Structures Unveiled

The mid-20th century brought about a linguistic revolution with Noam Chomsky's development of generative grammar. This theory proposed that innate cognitive structures in the human mind give rise to grammatical rules, fundamentally transforming our understanding of language.

Contemporary Approaches: Cognitive Linguistics and Beyond

In the present era, cognitive linguistics takes center stage, exploring the influence of cognition on grammatical structures. Researchers delve into how metaphor, conceptualization, and embodied cognition shape the very foundations of language.

Globalization of Grammar: English as a Lingua Franca

In the 21st century, grammar continues to evolve in a globalized world. English, as a prominent lingua franca, exerts influence on grammatical norms worldwide, reflecting the rich diversity of linguistic expressions in our interconnected world.

Conclusion: Grammar as a Living Entity

The journey of grammar is ongoing, adapting to technological advancements and reflecting the multifaceted expressions of human communication. Grammar remains a dynamic bridge connecting diverse cultures and linguistic traditions, contributing to the ever-evolving story of how we communicate and connect across borders.

Vocabulary

innate: Naturally present or inherent; something that is part of one's essential nature or abilities.

prescriptive: Relating to rules or guidelines dictating correct language usage; providing authoritative instructions on how something should be done.

vernacular: The everyday language spoken by ordinary people in a particular region or community, as opposed to a formal or literary language.

codification: The process of organizing laws, rules, or principles into a systematic and formal set of codes or regulations.

structuring: The act of arranging or organizing elements into a specific form or pattern.

revitalized: To bring something back to life, energy, or activity; to renew or reinvigorate.

formalization: The process of giving a formal or official structure to something, making it systematic or legally recognized.

departed: To deviate or move away from a previous practice or approach; to go in a different direction.

multifaceted: Having many different aspects, features, or perspectives; characterized by a variety of elements.

interconnected: Having connections or relationships between different parts; mutually related or dependent on each other.

Vocabulary Challenge

1. Bedrock, in the first paragraph is closest in meaning to:

   a) solid rock

   b) a foundation

   c) fundamental principle

   d) minerals

2. Dawn, in the second paragraph is closest in meaning to:

   a) the beginning

   b) the first appearance of light

   c) a time of the day

   d) the end

3. Clarity, in the third paragraph is closest in meaning to:

   a) confusion

   b) purity

   c) intelligible

   d) cleanliness

4. Elites, in the fourth paragraph is closest in meaning to:

   a) the rich

   b) the famous

   c) the educated

   d) the superior

5. Norms, in the fourth paragraph is closest in meaning to:

   a) a pattern

   b) something that is unusual

   c) how to act

   d) something unacceptable

Answers

   1. c

   2. a

   3. c

   4. d

   5. a

Multiple Choice Questions

1. What does the term "innate" mean in the context of language development?

   a) Learned through experience

   b) Naturally present or inherent

   c) Socially acquired

   d) Vernacular expression

2. In the Middle Ages, Latin became the standard language for:

   a) Everyday communication

   b) Vernacular literature

   c) Scholars and elites

   d) Descriptive grammar

3. What is the primary focus of prescriptive grammar manuals during the Middle Ages?

   a) Describing natural language usage

   b) Codifying vernacular languages

   c) Emphasizing "correct" language usage

   d) Analyzing linguistic structures

4. During the Renaissance, what contributed to the renewed interest in vernacular languages?

   a) Decline of written language

   b) Exploration of Latin

   c) Shift from Latin to vernacular languages

   d) Suppression of grammatical knowledge

5. What characterizes descriptive grammar as developed during the Enlightenment era?

   a) Prescribing language rules

   b) Focusing on innate cognitive structures

   c) Observing language in action

   d) Establishing a standard language

6. What is the key contribution of Ferdinand de Saussure to linguistics in the 19th century?

   a) Descriptive grammar principles

   b) Vernacular language analysis

   c) Exploration of deep language structures

   d) Codification of Latin grammar

7. What is the central idea behind Noam Chomsky's generative grammar?

   a) Language as a cultural construct

   b) Language evolves through experience

   c) Innate cognitive structures give rise to grammatical rules

   d) Language follows prescriptive norms

8. What does the term "cognitive linguistics" primarily emphasize in the study of grammar?

   a) Innate language structures

   b) Cultural influences on language

   c) Metaphors and conceptualization

   d) Formal grammatical rule

9. In the 21st century, English is considered a lingua franca. What does this mean?

   a) English is only spoken in France

   b) English serves as a global communication bridge

   c) English is a formal academic language

   d) English is limited to specific regions

10. What term describes the ongoing process of adapting grammar to technological advancements and reflecting diverse linguistic expressions?

    a) Descriptive grammar

    b) Innate language development

    c) Codification

    d) Grammar as a living entity

Answers

1. b

2. c

3. c

4. c

5. c

6. c

7. c

8. c

9. b

10. d

Day 17: Get Into Trouble

Ian is talking to Ted about his many problems on the weekend.

Ted: Hey Ian, how was your weekend?

Ian: Oh, I **got into trouble** again! I got a **parking ticket, got lost** while hiking and then maybe got **food poisoning**.

Ted: Oh wow. That sounds terrible. You always have interesting stories though, right?

Ian: I'm **envious of** your life. It seems much calmer.

Ted: Well, it's **not all rainbows and unicorns**. I **asked somebody out** but she rejected me. I'm thinking about **giving up** on dating altogether.

Ian: Hang in there my friend. There are **plenty of fish in the sea**.

Vocabulary

got into trouble: Had some problems happen.

parking ticket: A fine you have to pay for parking illegally.

got lost: Didn't know where you were.

food poisoning: Getting sick from something that you ate.

envious of: Jealous of.

not all rainbows and unicorns: Real life isn't as good as it appears to others.

asked somebody out: Asked someone if they wanted to go on a date.

giving up: Stop trying.

plenty of fish in the sea: There are many eligible people to date.

Practice

1. He _____ out hiking because he didn't have any extra clothes or food and then he got lost.

2. When was the last time you _____? Maybe that's why you don't have a girlfriend!

3. I _____ all the time when I was visiting Seoul. It's such a big city!

4. Do you think that maybe it's _____? Why don't you go to the ER?

5. I'm _____ Joe. He always seems to have so many ladies to go on dates with.

6. I'm thinking about _____ scuba diving. It's such an expensive hobby.

7. Things are not always as they appear. My life is _____.

8. I know you're sad but there are _____.

9. If you don't pay your _____ on time, the fine doubles after a month.

Answers

1. got into trouble

2. asked somebody out

3. got lost

4. food poisoning

5. envious of

6. giving up

7. not all rainbows and unicorns

8. plenty of fish in the sea

9. parking ticket

Day 18: Highly Effective

Jim and John are talking about managing money.

Jim: Hey John. I'm wondering how you and Tina manage your money? It's a **key issue** for Jen and I and we need to come up with a better system.

John: We've been **married for 20 years** now and have a **joint account**. What works for us is that we're **brutally honest** about what we spend our money on. We don't **keep secrets**.

Jim: You're married to a keeper. That's for sure. Jen is **between jobs** and I'm **worried sick** about it. We may have to **borrow money** from the bank to **pay the mortgage**.

John: Sorry to hear that. When **money was tight** for us, we found a **highly effective** budgeting system. It could work for you.

Vocabulary

key issue: The most important thing.

married for _____ years: Number of years after a wedding that two people are together.

joint account: A bank account that two or more people hold together.

brutally honest: Holding nothing back from each other; no secrets.

keep secrets: Not telling important information.

between jobs: Describes someone who lost a job but is looking for another one.

worried sick: Anxious or stressed out to the extreme.

borrow money: Get a loan.

money was tight: Not enough money.

highly effective: Describes something that works very well.

Practice

1. Tony and I have been _____.

2. Can I be _____ with you? This partnership just isn't working out for us.

3. I don't want to _____ from each other anymore. It makes our relationship difficult.

4. Tim always seems to be _____. I wonder what's up with him?

5. _____ when I was going to medical school.

6. I know that you're _____ about it but get some sleep.

7. I've heard that it's a _____ system for losing weight.

8. Why don't we open up a _____? It would make things easier.

9. Let's try to _____ to make it through these next few weeks.

Answers

1. married for 10 years

2. brutally honest

3. keep secrets

4. between jobs

5. money was tight

6. worried sick

7. highly effective

8. joint account

9. borrow money

Day 19: A Hiking Misadventure

Once upon a time, in a small town nestled between towering mountains, there lived a curious and adventurous young man named Jack. Jack had always been fascinated by nature and the great outdoors, so he decided to **embark** on a hiking adventure one sunny morning.

Armed with a backpack filled with snacks, a map, and his trusty compass, Jack set off on a trail that wound through the dense forest. The air was crisp, and the sound of birds chirping added to the **tranquil ambiance**. Jack was thrilled to explore new paths, discover hidden waterfalls, and breathe in the fresh mountain air.

As Jack ventured deeper into the woods, he became **enthralled** by the beauty surrounding him. The tall trees seemed to whisper ancient secrets, and the sunlight peeked through the canopy, creating a magical dance of light and shadows. However, in his excitement, Jack failed to notice that he had **deviated** from the main trail.

After a while, Jack realized that he couldn't find any familiar landmarks. His heart raced as panic began to set in. The forest suddenly seemed unfamiliar and vast. He checked his map, but the unfamiliar paths and dense foliage made it difficult to determine his exact location. The once inviting woods now felt like a maze closing in on him.

Trying to keep a level head, Jack remembered the lessons he had learned about staying calm when lost. He knew that panicking would only make matters worse. He took a deep breath and decided to retrace his steps, hoping to find the trail he had strayed from.

With each step, the forest seemed to grow darker and more intimidating. Jack's mind played tricks on him as the **rustling** leaves and distant animal sounds heightened his sense of unease. He tried to ignore the fear and focused on the task at hand.

Suddenly, Jack heard a faint sound in the distance. It was a gentle stream, babbling through the forest. His spirits lifted as he followed the sound, hoping it would lead him to a familiar place. And sure enough, after what felt like an eternity, he stumbled upon the familiar path, bathed in sunlight, with the stream flowing beside it.

Relieved, Jack let out a sigh of relief and **thanked his lucky stars**. He had learned a valuable lesson about the importance of staying alert and following the trail markers. As he made his way back to the town, he marveled at the beauty of the forest but also respected its unpredictable nature.

From that day forward, Jack never went hiking without a hiking buddy or a detailed trail guide. He shared his story with others, emphasizing the importance of being prepared and staying calm in challenging situations. And whenever he looked at the mountains, he couldn't help but feel a sense of gratitude for the adventure that had taught him so much.

Please remember Jack's story as you embark on your own journeys. Stay **vigilant**, be prepared, and most importantly, stay calm when faced with unexpected challenges. Happy hiking!

Vocabulary

embark: Start; begin.

tranquil ambiance: Peaceful, quiet surroundings.

enthralled: Deeply fascinated.

deviated: Moved or strayed from the original plan.

rustling: Moving.

thanked his lucky stars: Was appreciative of his good luck.

vigilant: Aware; focused.

Comprehension Questions

1. Was Jack prepared for the hike?
2. How did he get lost?
3. How did his feeling about the forest change once he realized he was lost?
4. How did he find his way back?
5. What lesson did Jack learn from this experience?

Answers

1. He was partly prepared—he had snacks, a map, and a compass.

2. He got lost because he was paying attention to other things—not where he was going.

3. Once he got lost, the forest changed from a beautiful place to one that was scary and intimidating.

4. He found a stream, which led him back to the hiking trail.

5. Jack now always goes hiking with a friend and has a detailed trail guide.

Let's Talk More

1. Have you ever gotten lost? Describe that experience.

2. Have you heard about the 10 essentials for when you go hiking? What are they? Look it up on Google if you don't know.

3. How well do you prepare for a hike or walk?

4. Are you the type of person who likes adventures like this? Or, do you prefer a calmer kind of life?

5. Do you think it would be easy to get lost like this person did when out hiking?

Day 20: Abandon the Plan

Keith and Cindy are talking about a product that their company makes.

Keith: What do you think about product ABC? Sales have been terrible.

Cindy: I know. I think we have to **abandon** it. Or, at least **suspend** production until we can **undertake** some research about why it failed so badly.

Keith: The **vision** was good. And the marketing plan was **impeccable**. It's strange that it went so badly. I wonder if something went wrong with the **execution**?

Cindy: It could be related to that. There was likely a **myriad** of problems that we have no idea about.

Keith: Ahhh, well, you can't win them all.

Cindy: You're right! I did have high hopes for this one though.

Vocabulary

abandon: Give up, let go of something.

suspend: Stop.

undertake: Take on, commit to something.

vision: Planning for the future.

impeccable: Without fault or flaw.

execution: Carrying out a plan.

myriad: Many, without number.

Practice

1. We can't _____ the plan just yet. Let's wait another week to see how it goes.

2. We had a good plan, but the _____ was poor.

3. What's your _____ for dinner tonight? BBQ maybe?

4. We need to _____ operations in Canada. We're losing too much money.

5. Jen has _____ taste. Why don't you get her to help you choose an outfit?

6. There is a _____ of reasons why you can't go, and I've already explained most of them to you.

7. Students are required to _____ simple experiments during the lab portion of this course.

Answers

1. abandon

2. execution

3. vision

4. suspend

5. impeccable

6. myriad

7. undertake

Day 21: Affordable Housing

Kerry and Joe are talking about how expensive housing is after their Sociology class.

Kerry: Did you hear that the city of Vancouver is **taking action** to address **housing prices**?

Joe: What are they doing? I'd love to move but **affordable housing** is hard to come by.

Kerry: I'm **in the same boat**. The city of Vancouver is building a new **housing development** and offering **low-interest rate** mortgages.

Joe: It's about time. Unless you **inherit money**, it's almost impossible for the **working Joe** to buy a house here.

Kerry: Well, **check into it** and if you buy a place, invite me to your **housewarming party**!

Vocabulary

taking action: Doing something.

housing prices: The average price of houses in an area.

affordable housing: Housing that is designed to be cheaper than normal, usually subsidized by the government.

in the same boat: To be in the same bad situation.

housing development: An area in which the houses have all been planned and built at the same time in an organized way.

low-interest rates: When interest rates are lower than normal.

it's about time: Finally.

inherit money: Receiving money that someone left you in their will.

working Joe: The average working person.

check into it: Find out more information about something.

housewarming party: A party to celebrate moving into a new home.

Practice

1. What are the average _____ in Victoria like?

2. Are you going to _____ when your parents die?

3. I'd love to get into that new _____ in the west end of the city.

4. I'm happy that the city is finally _____ on that guy across the street.

5. It's difficult for working families to buy a house in a place with no _____.

6. Congratulations on your new place! When's the _____?

7. Stop complaining. We're all _____.

8. Did he finally do his chores? _____.

9. I'm just an average _____, doing the 9-5.

10. I'm not sure about that. I'll have to _____.

11. It's a great time to buy a house when there are _____.

Answers

1. housing prices

2. inherit money

3. housing development

4. taking action

5. affordable housing

6. housewarming party

7. in the same boat

8. it's about time

9. working Joe

10. check into it

11. low-interest rates

Day 22: The Rise of Teotihuacán

The ancient city of Teotihuacán, nestled in the highlands of central Mexico, stands as a **testament** to the sophisticated and influential cultures that **flourished** in Mesoamerica centuries before the arrival of the Spanish conquistadors. The rise of Teotihuacán, often referred to as the "City of the Gods," is a captivating narrative that unveils the mysteries surrounding this archaeological **marvel**.

Foundations and Early Settlement

Teotihuacán's origins trace back to the Preclassic period (200 BCE - 200 CE), with evidence of small agricultural communities in the region. However, it wasn't until around 150 BCE that the first monumental structures began to emerge. The builders of Teotihuacán employed **innovative** construction techniques, creating impressive pyramids and structures that laid the foundation for the city's future greatness.

Urban Planning and Architecture

The most striking feature of Teotihuacán is its meticulously planned urban layout. The city covers over 20 square kilometers and is designed on a grid system, with the Avenue of the Dead serving as the central axis. Flanked by majestic pyramids and adorned with residential complexes and temples, this grand avenue reflects a deliberate and organized approach to city planning.

The Pyramid of the Sun, one of Teotihuacán's iconic structures, dominates the skyline. Rising to a height of approximately 75 meters, it stands as one of the largest pyramids in the ancient world. The Pyramid of the Moon, another prominent edifice, complements the grandeur of its counterpart, contributing to the overall symmetry and symbolism embedded in the city's architecture.

Cultural Significance and Influence

Teotihuacán's cultural influence extended far beyond its urban borders. The city became a **melting pot** of diverse Mesoamerican cultures, evident in its art, pottery, and murals. The famous "Mural of the Feathered Serpent" in the Temple of the Feathered Serpent (also known as the Temple of the Plumed Serpent) showcases intricate details and symbolic representations, offering insights into the cosmological beliefs and rituals of Teotihuacán's inhabitants.

The influence of Teotihuacán reached distant regions, as trade networks connected the city with other Mesoamerican civilizations. Artifacts discovered at archaeological sites across Mexico attest to the widespread impact of Teotihuacán's cultural and economic prowess.

Demography and Social Structure

Estimates suggest that at its zenith, Teotihuacán was home to a population ranging from 100,000 to 200,000 inhabitants, making it one of the most populous cities of its time. The demographic diversity is evident in the city's housing structures, which include apartment complexes and multi-story buildings. The social organization of Teotihuacán remains a subject of scholarly inquiry, with evidence suggesting a hierarchical structure led by a ruling elite.

Collapse and Theories of Decline

The decline of Teotihuacán is as enigmatic as its rise. Around 600 CE, the city underwent a series of transformations, marked by widespread destruction and abandonment. The reasons behind Teotihuacán's collapse remain speculative, with scholars proposing various theories, including internal unrest, social upheaval, environmental factors, or a combination of these elements.

One prevailing theory suggests that internal conflicts or external invasions might have led to the downfall of the once-thriving metropolis. The intentional destruction of key structures, such as the Feathered Serpent Pyramid, has fueled speculation about violent social unrest or ideological clashes.

Another perspective points to environmental factors, including drought or volcanic activity, disrupting agricultural practices and leading to resource scarcity. These environmental challenges could have triggered social instability and ultimately contributed to the city's abandonment.

Legacy and Archaeological Exploration

Despite its decline, Teotihuacán left an enduring legacy. The Aztecs, who arrived in the region centuries after Teotihuacán's collapse, regarded the city as a sacred site associated with the gods. They named it Teotihuacán, meaning "the place where the gods were created" in Nahuatl, the Aztec language.

Archaeological exploration of Teotihuacán began in the 19th century and continues to the present day. Excavations have unearthed residential areas, marketplaces, and ceremonial complexes, providing invaluable insights into the daily life, religious practices, and economic activities of the city's inhabitants.

Conclusion

The rise of Teotihuacán remains a compelling chapter in the annals of Mesoamerican history. This once-thriving metropolis, with its awe-inspiring architecture and cultural richness, continues to captivate the imagination of scholars and visitors alike. As researchers delve deeper into the mysteries of Teotihuacán, the city's legacy endures not only in the stones and structures that stand testament to its past glory but also in the ongoing quest to understand the complexities of this ancient marvel and the civilizations that called it home.

Vocabulary

archaeological: Relating to the study of past human societies and cultures through the excavation and analysis of artifacts, structures, and other physical remains.

cosmological: Pertaining to the study of the universe's origin, structure, and overall order, often involving religious or cultural beliefs about the cosmos.

hierarchical: Arranged in a system of levels or ranks, where each level is subordinate to the one above it, reflecting a structured and organized order.

symmetry: The quality of being made up of exactly similar parts facing each other or around an axis, creating balance and proportion in design or structure.

enigmatic: Mysterious, puzzling, or difficult to understand, often referring to something that arouses curiosity or intrigue due to its unclear nature.

zenith: The highest point or culmination, representing the peak or apex of a process, achievement, or celestial body's path in the sky.

prowess: Exceptional skill or ability, especially in a particular field or endeavor, showcasing high levels of competence or expertise.

ceremonial: Relating to formal or ritualistic observances, often associated with religious, cultural, or symbolic events.

annals: Historical records or accounts, often chronicling events in chronological order, providing a written narrative of significant occurrences over time.

Vocabulary Challenge

1. Testament, in the first paragraph is closest in meaning to:

    a) evidence

    b) related to the Bible

    c) a will

    d) a fact

2. Flourished, in the first paragraph is closest in meaning to:

    a) got smaller

    b) waving arms

    c) developed well

    d) moved around

3. Marvel, in the first paragraph is closest in meaning to:

    a) filled with anger

    b) filled with excitement

    c) a disappointing thing

    d) an impressive thing

4. Innovative, in the second paragraph is closest in meaning to:

    a) exciting

    b) well-tested

    c) featuring something new

    d) interesting

5. Melting pot, in the fifth paragraph is closest in meaning to:

    a) a place where people blend together well

    b) a place where people maintain their individual identities

    c) a pot where people make fondue

    d) a place where gold and silver are melted

Answers

    1. a

    2. c

    3. d

    4. c

    5. a

69

Multiple Choice Questions

1. What is the primary focus of archaeological studies?

   a) Analysis of climate patterns

   b) Exploration of ancient civilizations

   c) Observation of celestial bodies

   d) Examination of genetic codes

2. Which term refers to a structured system with levels or ranks, where each level is subordinate to the one above it?

   a) Symmetry

   b) Hierarchical

   c) Cosmological

   d) Archaeological

3. What does the term "cosmological" relate to in the context of ancient cultures?

   a) Urban planning

   b) Celestial bodies

   c) Agricultural practices

   d) Social hierarchies

4. In the context of architecture, what does "symmetry" refer to?

   a) A mysterious design

   b) Balanced proportions

   c) Formal rituals

   d) Skilled craftsmanship

5. Which word describes something that is mysterious and difficult to understand?

a) Prowess

b) Annals

c) Enigmatic

d) Zenith

6. What does the term "zenith" signify in the context of a celestial body's path?

a) The lowest point

b) The highest point

c) A circular path

d) The starting point

7. What is prowess in the context of a person's abilities?

a) A ceremonial practice

b) Exceptional skill or ability

c) Historical records

d) Urban planning

8. Which term refers to structured records chronicling events in chronological order?

a) Prowess

b) Annals

c) Symmetry

d) Zenith

9. What does the term "ceremonial" typically relate to?

a) Skilled craftsmanship

b) Ritualistic observances

c) Hierarchical structures

d) Celestial bodies

10. What is the primary focus of the field of archaeology?

a) Exploration of contemporary societies

b) Analysis of living organisms

c) Examination of ancient artifacts and structures

d) Observation of astronomical phenomena

Answers

1. b
2. b
3. b
4. d
5. c
6. b
7. b
8. b
9. b
10. c

Day 23: Break Up

Keith is talking to Carrie about breaking up with her boyfriend.

Carrie: Did you **break up** with Chris yet?

Keith: I was hoping you wouldn't ask me that question! I can't **go through with** it. I'm worried that he's going to be **pissed off** at me.

Carrie: You can **let him off** easily though, right? Be super kind. I know that you don't like **hanging around** with him.

Keith: It's true, yes. I need to **shake things up** and finally end it. Let me go do it right now before I **talk myself out of** it.

Vocabulary

break up: End a romantic relationship.

go through with: Do something that you have planned in advance.

pissed off: Be angry at someone or about something.

let him off: Release.

hanging around: Spending time with.

shake things up: Make a change.

talk myself out of: Convince yourself not to do something.

Practice

1. I think you should _____ with Tony. He's not a good guy!

2. Jay is _____ because I made him clean his room.

3. I have to not _____ asking women out. I just get so nervous

4. Sid and Jen are _____ together a lot these days. Maybe they'll start dating?

5. I'm not sure I can _____ the tattoo. It seems so painful.

6. We need to _____ a bit. Maybe we need to fire one of the low-performers?

7. I'm not sure you should _____ so easily. He needs some punishment for what he did. You don't always need to be the good guy.

Answers

1. break up

2. pissed off

3. talk myself out of

4. hanging around

5. go through with

6. shake things up

7. let him off

Day 24: The Fox and the Crow

In a serene forest, a **clever** fox and an **curious** crow lived amongst the trees. One day, the crow discovered a delectable piece of cheese and perched on a high branch to savor its find.

Observing the crow from a distance, the fox **hatched** a **cunning** plan. Approaching the crow with a smile, the fox spoke, "Greetings, noble crow! I've heard tales of your magnificent singing. Would you do me the honor of gracing the forest with your melodious voice?"

The crow, flattered by the fox's praise, eagerly opened its **beak** to sing. However, as the beautiful notes filled the air, the piece of cheese slipped from the crow's beak and fell to the ground below.

Seizing the opportunity, the fox swiftly grabbed the cheese, expressing gratitude, "Thank you, gracious crow! Your singing is as splendid as rumored." With the stolen prize in its jaws, the fox made a quick escape, leaving the crow bewildered and without its cherished cheese.

The moral of the story imparts a lesson about the danger of being easily swayed by **flattery**. The fox used charming words to deceive the crow and snatch the prize, emphasizing the importance of discernment and not letting sweet words cloud one's judgment.

The Moral

The moral of the story is to be careful and not believe everything people say, especially if they want something from you. It teaches us to be cautious and not let flattery or kind words cloud our judgment.

Vocabulary

beak: The nose of a bird.

clever: Smart; intelligent.

curious: Eager to know or learn about something.

flattery: Excessive praise.

hatched: Came up with.

cunning: Tricky; deceitful.

Comprehension Questions

1. Why did the fox approach the crow?
2. What did the fox compliment the crow on?
3. What did the crow do when the fox asked it to sing?
4. What happened while the crow was singing?
5. How did the fox get the cheese?

Answers

1. The fox approached the crow because it saw the crow with a piece of cheese and wanted to find a way to get it.
2. The fox complimented the crow on being a magnificent bird and suggested that it had heard the crow's singing was extraordinary.
3. The crow, flattered by the fox's words, opened its beak to sing.
4. While the crow was singing, the piece of cheese fell from its beak to the ground below.
5. The sly fox took advantage of the crow's singing, grabbed the fallen cheese, and thanked the crow before running away.

Day 25: Eating Habits

Sun and Todd are talking about New Year's resolutions.

Sun: Do you have a **New Year's resolution** planned for 2021?

Todd: A big one! I want to change my **eating habits** by not eating so much **junk food** and **processed food**. I'm going to focus on **home-cooked meals** and smaller **portion sizes**.

Sun: Mine is very similar. I'm not going to **go on a diet** but I want to eat a **balanced diet** with more **fruits and vegetables**. And I want to avoid the **second helpings**, especially at dinner. That's my **Achilles heel**.

Todd: We should **hold each other accountable**.

Sun: Great idea!

Vocabulary

New Year's resolution: Thing you resolve to do for the upcoming year.

eating habits: General way of eating (can be healthy or unhealthy).

junk food: Food that isn't healthy. For example, chips and candy.

processed food: Food that has been manufactured in some way. Often contains lots of sugar, fat and salt.

home-cooked meals: Food that you cook at home.

portion sizes: How much food you eat at one time.

go on a diet: Eat less or differently to try to lose weight.

balanced diet: A wide variety of healthy foods.

fruits and vegetables: Fruits and vegetables!

second helpings: Taking a second portion of a meal after finishing your first portion.

Achilles heel: A weakness in someone who is generally strong.

hold each other accountable: Check in with each other to help achieve some goal.

Practice

1. Let's _____ for this. I want to get this done under budget.
2. My son eats way too much _____. He probably eats an entire box of crackers a day!
3. I want to _____ so that I can lose weight for my sister's wedding.
4. His _____ is that he procrastinates.
5. Avoid _____ at dinner if you want to drop a few pounds.
6. I love _____ like potato chips and candy.
7. I want to reduce my _____. For example, only one piece of chicken instead of two.
8. It's best to eat a variety of brightly colored _____.
9. My _____ are terrible. I often skip breakfast and then snack late at night.
10. I love my husband's _____.
11. My _____ is to stop smoking.
12. A _____ consists of healthy foods from a variety of food groups.

Answers

1. hold each other accountable
2. processed food
3. go on a diet
4. Achilles heel
5. second helpings
6. junk food
7. portion sizes
8. fruits and vegetables
9. eating habits
10. home-cooked meals
11. New Year's resolution
12. balanced diet

Day 26: Monopoly

A professor is talking about monopolies in an Economics class.

These days, there aren't that many true monopolies except in government-owned companies like the post office, as well as water, gas, and electric companies. One of the best examples of a **monopoly** in **private industry** is Google which has **the upper hand** in the world of search. There are other **legitimate** competitors like Yahoo and Microsoft but they lag far behind in terms of market share and revenue.

Some people argue for government regulation of Google but others think that they shouldn't interfere. After all, Google provides a **superior** product and **consumers** are ultimately choosing to use them instead of someone else that also provides search results. Google has **state-of-the-art** servers and algorithms and seems to understand what people are looking for better than anyone else. **On the other hand**, companies like Yahoo maybe don't have **incentive** to improve their results because the gap between the two is **insurmountable**.

Vocabulary

monopoly: Only one company that offers a specific product or service.

private industry: A company that isn't run by the government.

the upper hand: Having power or control in a situation. Having an advantage.

legitimate: In this situation, refers to real or competitive.

superior: Better.

consumers: People who buy things or use services.

state-of-the-art: The best of something, usually related to technology.

on the other hand: To compare and contrast one idea or thing versus another.

incentive: Something that motivates or encourages someone to do something.

insurmountable: Can't be overcome.

Practice

1. The Smartphone industry is the opposite of a _____. There are many competitors.

2. Go in for the kill. You have _____.

3. I don't think healthcare should be delivered through _____.

4. There's no _____ to do well on the midterm exam. It's a pass-fail class.

5. You have a _____ concern but I think we can handle it.

6. The university just built an expensive, _____ research lab.

7. The US economy depends on _____ buying things.

8. Kate just got a C on her essay. _____, she did do well on that last project.

9. Learning a new language is not _____. The key is getting started.

10. Go with the pro model. It's more expensive but it's a _____ product.

Answers

1. monopoly

2. the upper hand

3. private industry

4. incentive

5. legitimate

6. state-of-the-art

7. consumers

8. on the other hand

9. insurmountable

10. superior

Day 27: Max and Emily

Once upon a time in a small town, there lived a young girl named Emily. Emily had a loyal and loving companion named Max, her faithful golden retriever. Max had been a part of Emily's life since she was a little girl, and they had shared countless joyful moments.

Max was not just a dog; he was Emily's best friend. They explored the neighborhood, **played fetch** in the park, and even cuddled up for bedtime stories. Max always seemed to understand Emily's emotions, providing comfort and **unconditional love** when she needed it most.

One sunny day, as Emily and Max were enjoying their usual afternoon walk, tragedy struck. Max suddenly collapsed, struggling to breathe. Alarmed and filled with worry, Emily quickly rushed him to the nearest veterinarian. The vet examined Max carefully and delivered heartbreaking news: Max's health had **deteriorated** rapidly, and there was little they could do to save him. Emily's heart sank with despair upon hearing the news.

Emily returned home, her heart heavy with grief. She sat on her bed, surrounded by Max's favorite toys and his worn-out dog bed. Tears streamed down her face as she **reminisced** about the countless memories she had shared with her beloved friend.

Days turned into weeks, and the emptiness in Emily's heart remained. She missed the sound of Max's paws on the floor, his wagging tail, and his warm presence beside her. Every corner of the house held a memory of him, and his absence felt unbearable.

Emily's parents understood her pain and decided to help her cope with the loss. They suggested creating a memory box for Max, filled with photographs, drawings, and heartfelt letters expressing their love and gratitude for him. They spent hours reminiscing about the happy moments they had shared with Max and remembering his playful antics.

Through the process of remembering and honoring Max, Emily and her family **found solace** in the memories they had created together. They celebrated Max's life, cherishing the love and joy he had brought into their lives. The memory box became a precious treasure, reminding them that Max would forever remain in their hearts.

As time passed, Emily's sorrow slowly transformed into acceptance and gratitude for the beautiful moments she had shared with Max. Though she missed him dearly, she knew that Max would want her to find happiness and love again.

One day, Emily's parents surprised her with a new puppy named Buddy. With a wagging tail and eyes full of curiosity, Buddy brought a newfound energy and excitement into their lives. Emily welcomed Buddy with open arms, understanding that while Max could never be replaced, her heart had room for new connections and love.

Emily and Buddy grew together, building their own unique bond. They embarked on new adventures, exploring the world with the same spirit of joy and love that Max had taught them. Max's memory continued to live on in their hearts, guiding them through life's ups and downs.

In the end, Emily realized that although saying goodbye to Max had been painful, his presence had forever changed her life for the better. Through love and memories, Max had taught her the true meaning of companionship and unconditional love, lessons that would stay with her forever.

And so, the tale of Emily, Max, and Buddy reminds us that even when we experience loss, the memories we create and the love we share can carry us through the darkest times, **illuminating** our path toward healing and happiness.

Vocabulary

played fetch: A game that humans and dogs play. The human throws a stick, the dog runs to get it and then brings it back.

unconditional love: Love that doesn't depend on anything.

deteriorated: Got worse.

reminisced: Remembered happy memories.

found solace: Found comfort.

illuminating: Lighting.

Comprehension Questions

1. Does Emily love Max?

2. Did Emily have Max for a long time?

3. What did Emily's family do to remember Max?

4. Who is Buddy?

5. Was Buddy going to replace Max?

Answers

1. Yes, she loves him. He is her best friend.

2. Yes, she did.

3. They made a memory box for Max.

4. Buddy is the new dog that Emily's parents got.

5. No. No dog could replace Max. But Emily could also love Buddy.

Let's Talk More

1. Have you ever had a pet that you really loved? Describe them.

2. Do people spend too much time and money on pets?

3. Should we euthanize pets that are very sick, or let them live as long as possible?

4. How can you choose a good pet that's suitable for you?

Day 28: Cajole

Tim is talking to his mom about his sister Emily.

Tim: Mom, why won't Emily talk to me?

Mom: Do you really not know? You're like a terrible **despot**!

Tim: What does despot mean?

Mom: A cruel ruler. You **cajole** and **connive** against her all the time.

Tim: So what should I do?

Mom: Well, if you want to **restore** your relationship, be nice to her. You can't **persist** in what you're doing and expect her to not hate you. **Appease** her when she asks you for a ride somewhere. **Acquiesce** when she wants to watch a TV show.

Tim: That sounds like a lot of work.

Vocabulary

despot: Cruel ruler.

connive: Plan or plot against someone or something.

cajole: Persuade someone to do something that they don't want to do.

restore: Repair, make whole again.

persist: Keep trying or going.

appease: Pacify or placate someone.

acquiesce: Give in.

Practice

1. Did you hear that the _____ of Country ABC just died?

2. You have to _____ the foundation before moving ahead with the rest of it.

3. My husband just won't _____ about buying a new car.

4. I feel like my boss often _____ against me. I'm not sure if it's all in my head though.

5. _____ with your course! You're almost done, right?

6. You can try to _____ Tommy, but I think he's already made up his mind.

7. Don't come if you're only doing it to _____ me. You'll be in a bad mood.

Answers

1. despot

2. restore

3. acquiesce

4. connives

5. persist

6. cajole

7. appease

Day 29: Darwin's Theory of Evolution

Charles Darwin's Theory of Evolution, presented in his **seminal** work "On the Origin of Species" in 1859, stands as a pivotal **milestone** in the history of biology. This groundbreaking theory reshaped our comprehension of life's origins and diversification, challenging prevailing beliefs and setting the stage for a unified framework in the biological sciences.

Natural Selection: The Engine of Evolution

At the core of Darwin's theory is the concept of natural selection, a mechanism that propels the gradual adaptation of species to their environment. Darwin observed the existence of variation in traits within populations and proposed that this diversity plays a crucial role in a species' ability to survive and reproduce. Natural selection acts as a selective force, favoring traits that **confer** advantages in the struggle for existence and gradually leading to the evolution of species over time.

Malthusian Influence: Population Dynamics in Nature

Darwin drew inspiration from the work of economist Thomas Malthus, who **posited** that human populations grow exponentially, leading to competition for limited resources. Darwin applied this principle to the natural world, suggesting that organisms, like human populations, face a constant struggle for existence. This struggle serves as the **crucible** in which natural selection operates, favoring traits that enhance an individual's chances of survival and reproduction.

Observations from the HMS Beagle: A Journey into Diversity

Darwin's voyage on the HMS Beagle provided him with a wealth of firsthand observations, particularly in the Galápagos Islands. These observations showcased variations in species adapted to different ecological niches, offering tangible evidence for the operation of natural selection. Additionally, his studies of domesticated plants and animals illuminated patterns of change over time, contributing to the formulation of his evolutionary theory.

Challenging Prevailing Beliefs: The Evolution-Religion Nexus

Darwin's theory challenged deeply rooted religious beliefs that advocated a fixed and unchanging creation. The concept of evolution by natural selection presented a dynamic and gradual process that contradicted traditional views. This clash between science and religious orthodoxy ignited controversy and resistance, marking a significant turning point in the relationship between science and faith.

Empirical Support and Interdisciplinary Corroboration

Over time, Darwin's theory garnered empirical support from diverse scientific disciplines. Fossil records provided evidence of transitional forms, while comparative anatomy and molecular biology revealed homologous structures and common ancestry among different organisms. Advances in genetics in the 20th century further solidified the molecular basis for evolutionary change.

Legacy and Beyond: Darwin's Lasting Impact

Darwin's Theory of Evolution transcended the realm of biology, sparking debates in ethics, philosophy, and theology. It influenced discussions on human nature, morality, and humanity's place in the natural world. As we unravel the mysteries of biology, Darwin's insights endure as a guiding beacon, emphasizing the dynamic and ever-evolving nature of life's interconnected tapestry.

Vocabulary

evolution: The process of gradual change over time, especially the development of species through natural selection.

natural selection: The mechanism by which certain traits within a population are favored over others, leading to the increased likelihood of those traits being passed on to future generations.

adaptation: The adjustment or modification of an organism's features or behaviors to suit its environment, enhancing its chances of survival and reproduction.

variation: Differences or diversity in traits observed among individuals within a population of organisms.

species: A group of organisms that share common characteristics and can interbreed to produce fertile offspring.

fossil records: Preserved remains or traces of ancient organisms found in rocks, providing insights into the history of life on Earth.

homologous structures: Similar anatomical structures found in different species, indicating a common evolutionary origin.

Malthusian: Relating to the ideas of Thomas Malthus, particularly the theory that population growth can outpace the availability of resources, leading to competition and natural selection.

empirical: Based on observation, experience, or evidence from the real world rather than theory or speculation.

paradigm shift: A fundamental change in a scientific theory or approach that results in a new way of understanding or explaining phenomena.

Vocabulary Challenge

1. Seminal, in the first paragraph is closest in meaning to:
   a) something related to plants
   b) something that strongly influences other things
   c) the first
   d) something new

2. Milestone, in the first paragraph is closest in meaning to:

   a) a stone that marks a mile in distance

   b) a method of punishment

   c) something significant

   d) the foundation of a building

3. Confer, in the second paragraph is closest in meaning to:

   a) have a discussion

   b) informal talk with friends

   c) bestow

   d) move

4. Posited, in the third paragraph is closest in meaning to:

   a) put forward as an argument

   b) factually proved

   c) put into position

   d) put money into the bank

5. Crucible, in the third paragraph is closest in meaning to:

   a) a glass or ceramic container

   b) a metal container

   c) a science laboratory

   d) a place where elements interact

Answers

   1. b

   2. c

   3. c

   4. a

   5. d

Multiple Choice Questions

1. What is the central concept of Darwin's Theory of Evolution?

   a) Genetic engineering

   b) Natural selection

   c) Artificial selection

   d) Genetic drift

2. Which scientist's work on population dynamics influenced Darwin's thinking about competition for resources?

   a) Albert Einstein

   b) Gregor Mendel

   c) Thomas Malthus

   d) Louis Pasteur

3. What term describes the gradual modification of an organism's features to suit its environment?

   a) Mutation

   b) Adaptation

   c) Hybridization

   d) Evolution

4. In the context of evolution, what does the term "variation" refer to?

   a) Differences in traits among individuals within a population

   b) Geographic distribution of a species

   c) The rate of mutation in a population

   d) The process of natural selection

5. What is the primary source of evidence supporting the theory of evolution from a historical perspective?

    a) Genetic sequencing

    b) Homologous structures

    c) Paleontological fossil records

    d) Artificial selection experiments

6. Which term describes structures in different species that share a common evolutionary origin?

    a) Analogous structures

    b) Homologous structures

    c) Vestigial structures

    d) Mutant structures

7. What was the groundbreaking work by Charles Darwin where he first presented his theory of evolution?

    a) Principles of Geology

    b) The Descent of Man

    c) The Voyage of the Beagle

    d) On the Origin of Species

8. Which term describes the process by which certain traits become more or less common in a population over generations due to random events?

    a) Genetic engineering

    b) Genetic drift

    c) Natural selection

    d) Artificial selection

9. In the context of evolution, what is the term for a group of organisms that can interbreed and produce fertile offspring?

    a) Genus

    b) Order

    c) Family

    d) Species

10. What does the term "paradigm shift" mean in the scientific context?

    a) A fundamental change in scientific theory or approach

    b) A temporary shift in climate patterns

    c) A sudden mutation in a population

    d) The introduction of a new species to an ecosystem

Answers

1. b
2. c
3. b
4. a
5. c
6. b
7. d
8. b
9. d
10. a

Day 30: Love at First Sight

Nancy is talking to Ethan about her new boyfriend.

Ethan: So, the **latest gossip** is that you have a new boyfriend.

Nancy: It's true. We were **casual acquaintances** but ran into each other again when a **mutual friend** had a **birthday party**.

Ethan: Exciting! That's great.

Nancy: He's **not my type** and it certainly wasn't **love at first sight** or anything like that. But, with time, I found that we had **strong chemistry**. **He's growing on me** more and more.

Ethan: Well, congratulations and I hope it goes well for you two.

Vocabulary

latest gossip: Most recent news, often involves details that aren't confirmed to be true.

casual acquaintances: Someone you know but aren't close friends with.

mutual friend: When two people share the same friend but aren't friends themselves.

birthday party: A celebration for someone's birthday.

love at first sight: A strong attraction from the first time meeting.

strong chemistry: A good connection between two people.

he's growing on me: You didn't initially like him that much but you like him more and more as you get to know him.

Practice

1. So, what's the _____ from the office? I've been away all week.

2. Jen and Kerry have _____ between them.

3. Are you going to Tom's _____ tonight?

4. Isn't Ted our _____?

5. Do you believe in _____?

6. I want to have more _____. I think I should join a club.

7. I didn't like him at first but now _____.

Answers

1. latest gossip

2. strong chemistry

3. birthday party

4. mutual friend

5. love at first sight

6. casual acquaintances

7. he's growing on me

Day 31: A Council of Mice

Once upon a time in a quiet meadow, there lived a **community** of mice. The mice were small but wise, and they had a leader named Whiskerington. One day, a group of mice noticed that the village cat, known as Whiskers, was catching more and more mice every day. The mice were frightened and didn't know what to do.

Feeling the need for a solution, the mice gathered for a **council** to discuss their predicament. Whiskerington, with his long whiskers and wise eyes, **presided** over the meeting.

A brave mouse named Squeaky spoke up first, "We must find a way to **outsmart** Whiskers and avoid being caught. Perhaps we can create a plan to **alert** each other when Whiskers is nearby."

Another mouse named Swift suggested, "What if we build safe **hiding spots** where we can quickly retreat if Whiskers comes too close?"

After much discussion, the council of mice decided to implement both ideas. They created a system of signals to warn each other about the cat's presence and built small, secure hiding places throughout the meadow. As days passed, the plan worked well, and the mice felt safer. Whiskers, no longer able to catch mice easily, grew frustrated and eventually gave up.

The moral of the story is that by working together and using their intelligence, the mice were able to overcome a common threat. It teaches us that unity and cleverness can overcome challenges, even when faced with a formidable opponent.

The Moral

The moral of the story is that when we work together and use our brains, we can solve problems and stay safe, even from something scary like a cat. Teamwork and clever thinking help us overcome challenges.

Vocabulary

hiding spots: Places where someone or something can't be found.

community: Group of people or animals.

council: Leaders or a group.

presided: Held a high position in a meeting.

outsmart: Defeat.

alert: Notify; tell.

Comprehension Questions

1. What was the problem that the mice faced in the story?
2. Who was the leader of the mice?
3. What were the two ideas the mice decided to use to stay safe from Whiskers?
4. Did the plan of the mice work against Whiskers? How?
5. What does the story teach us about solving problems?

Answers

1. The mice faced a problem of being caught by a cat named Whiskers.
2. Whiskerington was the leader of the mice.
3. The mice decided to warn each other when Whiskers was close and to build safe hiding spots.
4. Yes, the plan worked. By warning each other and having safe hiding spots, Whiskers couldn't catch the mice anymore.
5. The story teaches us that working together and using our brains can help us solve problems and stay safe.

Day 32: Wasting Time

Kim and Sally are talking about summer vacation plans.

Kim: What are you up to **this summer vacation**?

Sally: Oh, every summer, we head to our cabin at Lake Minnewanka.

Kim: Wow! I didn't know you had a cabin there.

Sally: Yeah, we bought it **5 years ago** and **since then**, have spent **as much time as possible** there. It's the perfect place for **wasting time**, doing almost nothing.

Kim: Well, you need to make time to relax, right? That sounds **idyllic.**

Sally: Definitely.

Kim: When are you heading out?

Sally: Actually, the **day after tomorrow**. I'm **under the gun** for packing!

Kim: Okay, have an awesome trip! Don't forget about your old friends **slaving away** at work.

Vocabulary

this summer vacation: Usually refers to time off that people have from school or work during July or August (in North America).

5 years ago: Now is 2021. 5 years ago = 2016.

since then: After a certain point in the past.

as much time as possible: The maximum amount, taking into account restrictions like school or work.

wasting time: Not doing much.

idyllic: Tranquil; peaceful.

day after tomorrow: In 2 days. For example, today is Monday. Day after tomorrow = Wednesday.

under the gun: Feeling pressure, usually due to a time constraint.

slaving away: Working hard.

Practice

1. _____, I've been doing way better.

2. I'm going to Japan the _____.

3. I've been _____ on this project for months now.

4. I graduated from high school _____.

5. _____ is what summer vacation is all about!

6. Let's find somewhere _____ to go to for vacation.

7. Can you stay late tonight? We're kind of _____ here.

8. _____, I'd love to finally read those books that have been sitting on my nightstand for months!

9. I try to spend _____ outside. It's great for my mental health.

Answers

1. since then

2. day after tomorrow

3. slaving away

4. 5 years ago

5. wasting time

6. idyllic

7. under the gun

8. this summer vacation

9. as much time as possible

Day 33: At Risk

Tom is talking to Jennifer about his sketchy coworker.

Jennifer: So, what's new at work?

Tom: Oh, I forgot to tell you. That guy Bob that I've mentioned before put our whole company **at risk**. Profits were **in decline**, but nobody could figure out why. It turns out our main competitor was paying him to sabotage the production line.

Jennifer: Oh wow. How did you figure it out?

Tom: Only **by luck.** We **speculated** he was the problem, but had no proof. We installed security cameras, but Bob didn't know about it. He got caught destroying a key piece of machinery.

Jennifer: Wow. He didn't act **in good faith**. But I guess there was no way to know that he'd go rogue at the outset.

Tom: Anyone can turn bad for enough money, I guess. It might be hard to **resist**.

Vocabulary

at risk: Exposed to harm.

in decline: Going down (often refers to health or financial things).

by luck: Success or failure caused by chance.

speculated: Formed a theory without evidence.

in good faith: With good intentions.

resist: Withstand.

Practice

1. That whole industry is _____. I wonder what happened?

2. I don't think things happen _____. All you need is hard work.

3. You can _____ anything if you put your mind to it.

4. That other company didn't negotiate _____.

5. We _____ for years about Bob and Cara, but they would never admit they were dating.

6. My business is _____ because I just lost a key employee.

Answers

1. in decline

2. by luck

3. resist

4. in good faith

5. speculated

6. at risk

Day 34: Hit the Books

Sam and Kara are talking about final exams that are coming up.

Sam: Are you ready for our chemistry **final**?

Kara: No, I have to **hit the books**. I'll probably **pull an all-nighter**, the night before.

Sam: You still have three more days to study. Why not start now? Pulling an all-nighter should be **the last resort**.

Kara: Oh, you know. I have to **get my act together** but I probably never will. I don't even have the latest **version** of the **textbook**. I hope it's the same material. It's **technical** stuff, so it should be fine I think.

Sam: **It begs the question**, what are you doing with your time if not studying like everyone else?

Kara: I'll never share my secrets. **That's another story**!

Vocabulary

final: Last. In this case, the exam at the end of a course.

hit the books: Study.

pull an all-nighter: Stay up all night to study.

the last resort: The last desperate thing someone does.

get my act together: Behave in a responsible manner after behaving badly.

version: A form of something, different from the earlier one.

textbook: A book used in a course.

technical: Usually refers to knowledge of machines or science.

It begs the question: Invites an obvious question.

that's another story: A phrase you can use to say that you don't want to talk about something that's been mentioned.

Practice

1. Isn't your _____ tomorrow? Why are you watching movies?

2. I only _____ once in university.

3. Which _____ are you using? It doesn't look the same as mine.

4. I hate asking Tina for help. It's _____ for me.

5. You're going to fail this class if you don't _____.

6. What? How much does that _____ cost? It's crazy!

7. I want to get into _____ writing. There's a weekend course I can take.

8. Well, _____. It's too long and complicated to tell you.

9. _____, why haven't we fired him? He's a terrible employee.

10. Sorry, I can't come. I have to _____. My test is tomorrow.

Answers

1. final

2. pulled an all-nighter

3. version

4. the last resort

5. get your act together

6. textbook

7. technical

8. that's another story

9. it begs the question

10. hit the books

Day 35: Ice Fishing in Manitoba

In the vast and frozen land of Manitoba, Canada lived a young man named Ethan. Ethan had always been fascinated by the icy wonders that surrounded him. He often heard tales of **ice fishing,** a popular activity in his community, and longed to experience it for himself.

One winter morning, Ethan woke up to find a **pristine** white blanket of snow covering the ground. The temperature had dropped significantly, and the nearby lakes had frozen over, signaling the perfect opportunity for him to fulfill his ice fishing dreams.

Excitedly, Ethan packed his warmest clothes, grabbed his fishing gear, and set off toward the frozen lake. As he arrived, he couldn't help but marvel at the winter landscape. The towering trees stood tall, their branches dusted with snow, while the sunlight danced on the sparkling ice.

Ethan carefully walked onto the frozen lake, ensuring each step was secure. He found a cozy spot and began to drill a hole through the ice. The sound of the drill echoed across the lake, making him feel like an explorer on a grand adventure.

With his fishing rod in hand, Ethan settled down, patiently waiting for a fish to bite. The air was crisp, and he could feel the cold seep into his bones. But the anticipation kept him warm. He watched as the line disappeared into the icy depths below, hoping for a tug that would signal a catch.

Time passed, and Ethan's patience started to waver. Just as he was about to give up, he felt a sudden jerk on his fishing line. His heart raced with excitement as he swiftly reeled in the fish. To his amazement, a beautiful **walleye** emerged from the icy hole.

Overjoyed, Ethan carefully removed the hook from the fish's mouth and marveled at its shimmering scales. He couldn't help but appreciate the stunning creature that lay before him. Grateful for the experience, he gently released the walleye back into the water, knowing that it would continue its journey beneath the frozen surface.

As the day went on, Ethan had more success with his ice fishing endeavors. Each catch brought him a sense of fulfillment and wonder. He even met fellow ice fishermen, who shared stories of their adventures and tips for success.

As the sun began to set, casting **hues** of orange and pink across the **horizon**, Ethan knew it was time to leave. Reluctantly, he packed up his gear, taking one last look at the frozen lake that had provided him with an unforgettable experience.

With a smile on his face, Ethan **trudged** through the snow, feeling a sense of accomplishment and connection to the winter world around him. He knew that he would always cherish the memories he had made while ice fishing in Manitoba.

And so, as the stars twinkled above, Ethan walked home, his heart filled with the beauty of nature and the joy of a dream fulfilled. Little did he know that this would be the first of many adventures on the ice, as he had discovered a love for ice fishing that would continue to warm his spirit for years to come.

Vocabulary

ice fishing: Catching fish under the ice by drilling a hole.

pristine: Untouched; unspoiled.

walleye: A kind of freshwater fish.

hues: Shades of color.

horizon: The line where the Earth and the sky appear to meet.

trudged: Walked slowly.

Comprehension Questions

1. Is Ethan new to Canada?
2. Do you think that Ethan fishes in the summertime?
3. Did Ethan give up hope on catching a fish?
4. Did he eat the fish he caught for dinner?
5. Will he go ice fishing again?

Answers

1. No, it seems like he's been living in Manitoba for a while. He's just never been ice fishing before.

2. He likely fishes in the summer. He has all the equipment and seems to know how to fish.

3. Yes, a little bit. His patience started to waver.

4. No, he released it back into the lake.

5. Yes, he will have many more fishing adventures on the ice.

Let's Talk More

1. Have you ever been fishing? What was that experience like?

2. Do you think ice fishing would be fun? Why or why not?

3. Do you prefer to be somewhere hot or cold?

4. Is fishing cruel to animals? What about catching them and then releasing them back, instead of eating them?

5. What are some other hobbies or sports that you can only do in certain climates?

Day 36: Dumped

Alex got dumped by his girlfriend.

John: Hey **bro**, what's up? You don't look so good.

Alex: I just got **dumped** by Kendra. And just when we started talking about **getting hitched.**

John: Sorry to hear that. Wasn't she super **flakey** though, always cancelling at the last minute?

Alex: Yeah, and I **straight up** caught her lying to me more than a few times.

John: Better off without her. Let's get **ripped** this weekend. It'll take your mind off of it.

Alex: Yeah, I want to **blow off some steam**. Just don't post about it on social media. I don't want to get **busted** by my boss. He just **added me** as a friend on Facebook.

Vocabulary

bro: A way to greet a close male friend (if you're also a guy).

dumped: Broken up with.

getting hitched: Getting married.

flakey: Describes someone who doesn't follow through with what they say or always cancels plans.

straight up: Speaking honestly.

ripped: Drunk.

blow off some steam: Relax; let loose.

added me: Becoming friends with someone on social media.

Practice

1. What do you like to do to _____?

2. I'll never work on another project with her if I can avoid it. She's so _____.

3. I got _____ last night at the work Christmas party. I hope that I didn't do anything too embarrassing.

4. Did you hear that Ted _____ Lindsay?

5. My grandma just _____ on Instagram. It's so cute!

6. I _____ never want to talk to that guy again.

7. Tom and I are _____ next month.

8. Hey _____, how are you doing these days?

Answers

1. blow off some steam

2. flakey

3. ripped

4. dumped

5. added me

6. straight up

7. getting hitched

8. bro

Day 37: The Nile River

The Nile River, often hailed as the **lifeblood** of northeastern Africa, weaves through the tapestry of the continent, leaving an indelible mark on the landscapes it traverses. Spanning approximately 6,650 kilometers (4,130 miles), the Nile stands as the longest river in the world, an ancient watercourse that has profoundly shaped the histories, cultures, and ecosystems of the diverse nations it touches. This majestic river holds a mystique that transcends geographical boundaries, embodying both the **cradle** of ancient civilizations and a contemporary source of vitality for the millions who depend on its waters.

Originating in the Heart of Africa

The Nile's journey begins deep in the heart of Africa, where its two main tributaries, the White Nile and the Blue Nile, converge in Khartoum, Sudan. The White Nile, originating from Lake Victoria, and the Blue Nile, rising from Lake Tana in Ethiopia, join forces to create the mighty Nile River, a confluence that marks the commencement of its extraordinary **odyssey**. From this point onward, the river winds its way northward, sculpting landscapes and nurturing a myriad of life forms along its course.

Historical Significance

The Nile is not merely a geographical feature; it is a historical tapestry woven into the narratives of ancient civilizations. Egypt, often regarded as the gift of the Nile, owes its prosperity to the annual flooding of the riverbanks, a natural phenomenon that **replenished** the soil with nutrient-rich sediments, fostering fertile lands along the Nile Delta. The ancient Egyptians recognized the cyclical nature of the river's flooding and developed sophisticated agricultural practices that allowed their civilization to thrive for millennia.

Beyond Egypt, the Nile also played a **pivotal** role in the development of Nubian and Sudanese civilizations. The river served as a lifeline for trade, communication, and sustenance, connecting communities along its banks and facilitating cultural exchanges that enriched the diverse tapestry of the region.

Ecosystem Diversity

The Nile River basin encompasses a remarkable diversity of ecosystems, ranging from dense tropical rainforests in its upper reaches to arid deserts in the north. This ecological richness has made the Nile a haven for a wide array of plant and animal species, many of which are endemic to the region. The river supports a wealth of biodiversity, from the iconic Nile crocodile and the elusive manatee to a plethora of bird species that thrive along its shores.

Contemporary Importance

In the 21st century, the Nile remains an indispensable resource for the countries through which it flows. The river serves as a source of water for agriculture, industry, and domestic use, sustaining the livelihoods of millions. However, the allocation and management of the Nile's waters have also been a source of contention among the riparian states, highlighting the complex geopolitical dynamics intertwined with this vital waterway.

As the Nile continues to flow through the annals of time, its significance persists, evolving to meet the needs of a changing world. The river's storied past, ecological diversity, and contemporary importance underscore its status as not just a geographic feature but a cultural, historical, and economic force that binds the destinies of the nations it touches. In the following exploration, we will delve deeper into the various facets of the Nile, unraveling its mysteries and appreciating its profound impact on the past, present, and future of northeastern Africa.

Vocabulary

confluence: The point at which two rivers or streams meet and flow together.

sediments: Particles of solid material, such as sand or soil, that settle at the bottom of a liquid, often carried by water.

cyclical: Occurring in cycles or repeated patterns.

riparian: Relating to or situated on the banks of a river or other body of water.

endemic: Native to a specific region and found nowhere else.

biodiversity: The variety of plant and animal life in a particular habitat or ecosystem.

geopolitical: Relating to the political and territorial relations between countries.

riparian states: Countries or regions that are located along the banks of a river or other body of water.

fertile: Capable of producing abundant vegetation or crops; rich in nutrients.

annals: Historical records or accounts, often in chronological order, detailing events and developments.

Vocabulary Challenge

1. Lifeblood, in the first paragraph is closest in meaning to:

    a) blood of humans or animals

    b) something large

    c) something unnecessary

    d) something indispensable

2. Cradle, in the first paragraph is closest in meaning to:

    a) move side to side

    b) where a baby sleeps

    c) a place where something begins

    d) where a ship rests out of the water

3. Odyssey, in the second paragraph is closest in meaning to:

    a) a long journey

    b) a famous book

    c) the beginning of something

    d) the end of something

4. Replenished, in the third paragraph is closest in meaning to:

    a) started over

    b) depleted

    c) filled something up again

    d) took something away

5. Pivotal, in the fourth paragraph is closest in meaning to:

    a) what athletes do

    b) changing direction

    c) somewhat important

    d) of crucial importance

Answers

    1. d

    2. c

    3. a

    4. c

    5. d

Multiple Choice Questions

1. What is the primary source of the Nile River?

   a) Lake Tanganyika

   b) Lake Victoria

   c) Lake Malawi

   d) Lake Chad

2. Which two tributaries converge to form the Nile River in Khartoum, Sudan?

   a) White Nile and Niger River

   b) Blue Nile and Congo River

   c) White Nile and Blue Nile

   d) Blue Nile and Zambezi River

3. What ancient civilization is often referred to as the "gift of the Nile"?

   a) Mesopotamia

   b) Indus Valley Civilization

   c) Ancient Greece

   d) Ancient Egypt

4. What natural phenomenon contributed to the fertility of the soil along the Nile Delta in ancient Egypt?

   a) Volcanic eruptions

   b) Annual flooding

   c) Earthquakes

   d) Desertification

5. Which term describes the point at which two rivers meet and flow together?

  a) Confluence

  b) Tributary

  c) Estuary

  d) Delta

6. What term is used to describe species that are native to a specific region and found nowhere else?

  a) Invasive

  b) Indigenous

  c) Endemic

  d) Exotic

7. What do you call the countries or regions located along the banks of a river or other body of water?

  a) Aquatic States

  b) Coastal Nations

  c) Riparian States

  d) Hydro States

8. What is the ecological term for the variety of plant and animal life in a particular habitat or ecosystem?

  a) Ecosystem Diversity

  b) Habitat Variation

  c) Biological Disparity

  d) Faunal Spectrum

9. What is the approximate total length of the Nile River?

   a) 3,000 kilometers

   b) 4,500 miles

   c) 5,800 kilometers

   d) 6,650 kilometers

10. How has the geopolitical significance of the Nile River led to contemporary challenges among riparian states?

   a) Shared management strategies

   b) Disputes over water rights

   c) Joint ecological conservation efforts

   d) Cultural exchange programs

Answers

   1. b

   2. c

   3. d

   4. b

   5. a

   6. c

   7. c

   8. a

   9. d

   10. b

Day 38: Empirical Evidence

Tommy and Sam are talking about climate change.

Tommy: Why does Professor Kim keep talking about **climate change** in his class? It's always **doom and gloom**. The **empirical evidence** to support it isn't that strong.

Sam: Oh, I totally disagree with you. The Earth is getting warmer and it's likely **irreversible** at this point. There's so much **evidence**. We can't **sustain** our current habits.

Tommy: Oh, we can just **innovate** our way out of it, don't you think?

Sam: **On the face of it,** science may help us a little bit but my **prediction** is that life as we know it will be over in 100 years or less if we don't **shift gears** in a radical way. Anyone can **infer** that it's just going to get worse in the future.

Vocabulary

climate change: The Earth getting warmer as a result of humans.

doom and gloom: A negative way of looking at things.

empirical evidence: Usually scientific knowledge gained by observation or experimentation.

irreversible: Can't be changed back.

evidence: Facts that prove something is true.

sustain: Support.

innovate: Make something new.

on the face of it: Without knowing all the facts or the complete picture.

prediction: A guess about the future.

shift gears: Change speed/direction or course or action.

infer: A guess or prediction based on evidence and reason.

Practice

1. I think that _____ is the biggest issue facing our world today.

2. The Earth can only _____ our current habits for another decade or two.

3. We need to _____ to save the Earth.

4. Climate change is probably _____ at this point.

5. You need to support your argument with some _____.

6. You can't _____ fast enough to reverse this issue.

7. The _____ supporting that climate change is real is so strong. Who could deny it?

8. What's your _____ for the final exam? A? B? C?

9. _____, it looks like it was Ted's fault.

10. I don't know for sure, but I can _____ that it's going to be a future problem.

11. Sorry to be all _____ about the environment. But, there's really no good news.

Answers

1. climate change

2. sustain

3. shift gears

4. irreversible

5. empirical evidence

6. innovate

7. evidence

8. prediction

9. on the face of it

10. infer

11. doom and gloom

Day 39: Brash and Aggressive

Kevin and Sandy are talking about one of Keith's classmates.

Sandy: How are your classes this semester?

Keith: Oh, they're fine, except for my political science class. There's one student that I **despise**.

Sandy: What does he do?

Keith: Well, he's so, **brusque**, **brash,** and **aggressive**. He'll say anything to anyone, and he **brags** about how much he knows. I'm certainly not **accustomed to** that.

Sandy: What does the professor do?

Keith: He doesn't **conceal** his dislike but not much besides that. I don't think he likes **conflict**. And this student is so **adamant** about what he thinks that I don't think anything the professor might say could change his mind.

Vocabulary

despite: Strong hate.

brusque: Abrupt to the point of rudeness.

brash: Rude, loud, in your face.

aggressive: Assertive or pushy.

brags: Boasts.

accustomed to: Used to something.

conceal: Hide.

conflict: Disagreement.

adamant: Refuse to change an opinion.

Practice

1. Believe it or not, I don't _____ him. I know it's hard to understand.

2. If you beat your brother at a game, be a good winner and don't _____ about it.

3. I was sure she was lying but she was so _____ that she wasn't.

4. We need to _____ this. I don't want the media to get wind of it.

5. Keith and I have so much _____. I think we need to break up.

6. Play hard but don't be too _____, or nobody will want to play with you.

7. Toby is kind of _____, but everyone puts up with him because he's a hard worker.

8. Running is fine if you're _____ it. It's just difficult starting out.

Answers

1. despise

2. brag

3. adamant

4. conceal

5. conflict

6. aggressive

7. brash/brusque

8. accustomed to

Day 40: Caught a Cold

Anita is talking to Ted about how she's not feeling well.

Ted: Hey Anita, what's up?

Anita: I've had a rough **couple of weeks**. I **caught a cold** and it took me a while to recover. I was just **getting ready** for Christmas too. It was **terrible timing**.

Ted: Oh no! Did you go to the doctor?

Anita: Yes, she said to take some **over-the-counter medications** because it was a virus.

Ted: Well, that's better than **taking antibiotics** when you don't need to. I think that happens **quite often** but it's certainly not a good thing.

Anita: Enough about me. How are you?

Ted: Well, I **had the flu** last month and I'm just **fully recovered** now.

Vocabulary

couple of weeks: Two weeks.

caught a cold: Got sick with a cold.

getting ready: Preparing.

terrible timing: A bad time for something negative to happen.

over-the-counter medications: Medicine that doesn't require a prescription.

taking antibiotics: Taking medicine that kills harmful bacteria.

quite often: Happens frequently.

enough about me: I've been talking too much about myself!

had the flu: Was sick with the flu but okay now.

fully recovered: Not sick anymore.

Practice

1. I was sick for almost a month but I'm now _____.

2. My son _____ from the other kids at school.

3. I _____ for almost two months. It was terrible.

4. Well, _____. What's happening with you these days?

5. He is _____ late for work.

6. These _____ have been tough. I lost my job plus my dog died too.

7. That's _____ for getting sick. November is your busiest month at work, right?

8. I've been _____ for my ear infection but it's not getting better.

9. I'm well stocked with _____ at home.

10. _____ for work takes me at least an hour.

Answers

1. fully recovered

2. caught a cold

3. had the flu

4. enough about me

5. quite often

6. couple of weeks

7. terrible timing

8. taking antibiotics

9. over-the-counter medications

10. Getting ready

120

Day 41: The Frightened Lion

Once upon a time in the heart of a vast **savanna**, there lived a powerful but frightened lion named Leo. Despite being the king of the jungle, Leo was afraid of many things. He feared the buzzing bees, the crackling thunderstorms, and even the tiny mice.

One day, Leo's animal friends gathered around him and noticed his anxious demeanor. A wise old elephant named Ella spoke up, "Leo, you are the **mightiest** lion in the jungle. Why do you let fear control you?"

Leo sighed and confessed, "I may be strong, but many things scare me. The buzzing of bees makes me nervous, the thunderstorms make me tremble, and even the smallest mice make me jump."

The animals decided to help Leo overcome his fears. They began with the buzzing bees. Slowly, Leo approached a beehive with the guidance of his friends. The bees, busy with their work, paid him no attention. Leo realized they were not interested in harming him.

Next, they faced the thunderstorms. The animals huddled together, and Leo learned that the thunder was just nature's way of making noise. The storm passed, and Leo felt a sense of relief.

Lastly, the mice. Leo's friends took him to meet a group of mice, and he saw they were more scared of him than he was of them. Leo realized that his fears were **unfounded**, and he felt a newfound confidence.

Leo thanked his friends for helping him **conquer** his fears. From that day on, he roared with strength, unburdened by unnecessary fears. The jungle celebrated the transformation of the once-frightened lion into a courageous and confident king.

The Moral

The moral of the story is that sometimes things that seem scary are not really as big as we think. With help from friends, we can be brave and face our fears.

Vocabulary

savannah: Grassland with few trees.

mightiest: The biggest.

unfounded: No foundation or basis in fact.

conquer: Overcome.

Comprehension Questions

1. What scared Leo the lion in the story?

2. Who noticed that Leo was always scared?

3. How did Leo's friends help him face his fear of bees?

4. What did Leo learn about thunderstorms with the help of his friends?

5. What made Leo feel braver in the end?

Answers

1. Leo was scared of buzzing bees, loud thunderstorms, and tiny mice.

2. Leo's friends, the other animals in the jungle, noticed that he was always scared.

3. They showed Leo that bees are busy and won't bother him if he doesn't bother them.

4. Leo learned that thunderstorms are just loud noises and not something to be afraid of.

5. Leo felt braver in the end because his friends showed him that the things he was scared of were not as big as he thought, and with their help, he could be strong and confident.

Day 42: Finishing Work for the Day

Jerry and Linda are going to get some dinner after work.

Jerry: I'm so tired. Let's **call it a day** and grab some dinner. It's **my treat**.

Linda: Sure, I'd love to but only if we **go Dutch**. You **foot the bill** for me too often!

Jerry: Sure, if you insist. Let's check out that dessert place. They have sandwiches and then I can satisfy my **sweet tooth**. It's expensive but **worth it** I think.

Linda: Okay, **twist my arm**. Let's go. And don't just pick up the bill when I'm in the bathroom. I want to **pony up** for my share, okay?

Jerry: Let's **make a break for it** before **the big cheese** finds more work for us to do!

Linda: Sure, let's **head out.**

Vocabulary

call it a day: To stop working for the rest of the day.

foot the bill: To pay for.

go Dutch: Each person pays their own bill, especially at a restaurant or bar.

pony up: To get money/credit cards out to pay for something.

worth it: Good enough to justify the high cost.

twist my arm: Convince to do something.

sweet tooth: To like sugary foods.

my treat: To offer to pay, usually for a meal or drink.

make a break for it: Leave somewhere quickly.

the big cheese: The boss.

head out: To go somewhere.

Practice

1. I feel uncomfortable when guys pay for me so I insist that we _____.

2. It's time to _____ for all those drinks you had!

3. I have a wicked _____ and can't stop eating candy.

4. Is the company going to _____ for the Christmas party this year?

5. Let's _____. I'm beat.

6. It's time to _____ and go home while the boss isn't looking.

7. Let's grab lunch. _____.

8. I hope to be _____ one day!

9. I'm tired. I'm going to _____ now.

10. Okay, I know that subscription box is expensive but it's _____ to me.

11. I didn't want to do it! My wife had to _____ to get me to go skydiving with her.

Answers

1. go Dutch

2. pony up

3. sweet tooth

4. foot the bill

5. call it a day

6. make a break for it

7. my treat

8. the big cheese

9. head out

10. worth it

11. twist my arm

Day 43: Burning the Midnight Oil

Jerry and Larry are talking about being very busy.

Jerry: I have to **hit the sack**. I'm so tired right now.

Larry: Have you been **burning the midnight oil** lately?

Jerry: Yeah, I've been trying to study for this test. I should have started earlier. My **tradition** is to wait until the last minute but it's not working for me in this case.

Larry: Well, **better late than never**. But, make sure to get enough sleep. If you're tired, you won't remember anything.

Jerry: You're right. It was **many moons ago** that I got a decent night's sleep.

Larry: Don't give up. I think you'll **ace** it. You're not **starting from scratch.** You already know lots of the material from that class you took last year, right? **It stands to reason** that you could probably get a decent mark without that much studying.

Jerry: It's true. Well, time to **knuckle down** and get to work.

Vocabulary

hit the sack: Go to bed.

burning the midnight oil: Staying up late working or studying.

tradition: A usual, historical way of doing things.

better late than never: Encouragement after getting a late start to something.

many moons ago: A long time ago.

ace: To get a high mark on a test or do well at something like a job interview.

starting from scratch: Starting from nothing or at the beginning.

it stands to reason: A reasonable deduction or conclusion.

knuckle down: To work very hard on something.

Practice

1. Don't forget to _____ early. It's your final exam tomorrow!

2. It was _____ that I was a student. I graduated in 2004.

3. I've been _____ lately, studying and working too. I need some more coffee.

4. Honestly, it's _____ but he dropped the ball on this project by waiting so long.

5. You won't _____ the test unless you study.

6. It's _____ that I wear my lucky hat for tests.

7. I'm _____ when it comes to computer stuff. It feels like learning the ABC's.

8. _____ that you'll get a raise this year. How could they not after your last project?

9. It's the last thing I want to do but I know it's time to _____ and study.

Answers

1. hit the sack
2. many moons ago
3. burning the midnight oil
4. better late than never
5. ace
6. tradition
7. starting from scratch
8. it stands to reason
9. knuckle down

Day 44: Hand Preference

Hand preference, often colloquially referred to as "handedness," is a fascinating aspect of human behavior that reflects the dominance of one hand over the other in performing various tasks. While the majority of individuals exhibit a clear preference for either the right or left hand, the underlying mechanisms and the factors influencing hand preference remain subjects of ongoing scientific inquiry.

Biological Foundations

The roots of hand preference can be traced to the **intricate** interplay between genetics and brain lateralization. Studies have suggested a genetic component, indicating that the inclination to favor one hand over the other may be hereditary to some extent. Identical twins, who share nearly identical genetic material, are more likely to have similar hand preferences than non-identical twins or non-related individuals. However, the genetic influence is not **absolute**, as environmental factors also play a crucial role in shaping hand preference.

The brain's lateralization, where certain functions are localized to specific hemispheres, contributes significantly to hand preference. In most right-handed individuals, the left hemisphere of the brain controls language and motor functions, leading to the dominance of the right hand in various tasks. Conversely, left-handed individuals often exhibit a more balanced distribution of functions between the hemispheres or even a dominance of the right hemisphere.

Developmental Patterns

Hand preference begins to **manifest** during infancy, with infants as young as six months displaying a tendency to reach for objects with a preferred hand. As children grow, their hand preference becomes more pronounced, with many establishing a clear preference by the age of three or four. Interestingly, the transition from an initial lack of hand preference to the establishment of a dominant hand is a **dynamic** process influenced by environmental stimuli and neurological maturation.

Cultural and societal factors also contribute to the development of hand preference.

In many societies, right-handedness is the predominant **norm**, leading to a higher prevalence of right-handed individuals. This prevalence is not universal, and certain cultures exhibit a higher proportion of left-handed individuals. These variations highlight the complex interplay between biological predispositions and cultural influences.

Left-Handedness

Left-handed individuals, constituting roughly 10% of the population, have historically been subjects of intrigue and, at times, social stigma. Throughout history, left-handedness has been associated with superstitions and negative connotations. The term "sinister," derived from the Latin word for left, reflects the historical bias against left-handedness. However, societal attitudes have evolved, and contemporary perspectives recognize left-handedness as a natural and diverse aspect of human behavior.

The neurological basis for left-handedness is not fully understood, but it is believed to result from a combination of genetic and environmental factors. Some left-handed individuals may have a family history of left-handedness, suggesting a genetic predisposition. Environmental factors, such as exposure to certain hormones during fetal development, may also contribute to the development of left-handedness.

Ambidexterity

While most individuals exhibit a clear hand preference, some people display a degree of ambidexterity, the ability to use both hands with equal skill. True ambidexterity, where both hands are equally dominant, is relatively rare. In many cases, individuals may show ambidextrous tendencies for specific tasks while maintaining a clear overall hand preference. The development of ambidexterity is influenced by both genetic factors and deliberate practice in using both hands.

Conclusion

In conclusion, hand preference is a multifaceted phenomenon shaped by genetic, neurological, developmental, and cultural factors. While the majority of individuals exhibit a clear preference for one hand, the diversity of hand preferences, including left-handedness and ambidexterity, adds a rich layer to the complexity of human behavior. As our understanding of the brain and genetics continues to advance, the exploration of hand preference offers insights into the intricacies of human development and the interplay between nature and nurture in shaping individual characteristics.

Vocabulary

lateralization: The specialization of functions in the left or right hemisphere of the brain.

genetics: The study of heredity and the variation of inherited characteristics.

ambidexterity: The ability to use both hands with equal skill.

hereditary: Passing of genetic traits or characteristics from parent to offspring.

superstitions: Beliefs or practices resulting from irrational fear of the unknown or unexplainable.

neurological: Pertaining to the nervous system, especially the brain and nerves.

predisposition: A tendency or inclination toward a particular condition or behavior.

norm: A standard or pattern that is considered typical or usual within a society or group.

stigma: A mark of disgrace or shame associated with a particular quality or characteristic.

intricate: Complicated, detailed, and complex in structure or design.

Vocabulary Challenge

1. Intricate, in the second paragraph is closest in meaning to:

    a) complicated

    b) confusing

    c) having many, interrelated parts

    d) too detailed to understand

2. Absolute, in the second paragraph is closest in meaning to:

    a) the only thing

    b) a moral principle

    c) inflexible

    d) a brand of Vodka

3. Manifest, in the fourth paragraph is most closely related to:

    a) a political idea

    b) obvious

    c) the appearance of a ghost or spirit

    d) show

4. Dynamic, in the fourth paragraph is most closely related to:

    a) a positive attitude

    b) changing

    c) related to electronics

    d) related to the volume of sound produced

5. Norm, in the fifth paragraph is most closely related to:

    a) short for "normal"

    b) typical or standard

    c) something that must always be done

    d) a mathematical term

130

Answers

1. c

2. a

3. d

4. b

5. b

Comprehension Questions

1. What is lateralization in the context of hand preference?

   a) The dominance of one hand over the other

   b) The ability to use both hands equally

   c) The specialization of functions in the brain hemispheres

   d) The influence of cultural factors on hand use

2. Which term refers to the passing of genetic traits from parent to offspring?

   a) Ambidexterity

   b) Lateralization

   c) Hereditary

   d) Predisposition

3. What does the term "ambidexterity" describe?

   a) The dominance of one hand over the other

   b) The ability to use both hands equally

   c) The preference for using the left hand

   d) The inclination to use the right hand

4. What does the term "hereditary" mean in the context of hand preference?

    a) Passing of genetic traits

    b) Cultural influence on hand use

    c) Environmental factors affecting hand preference

    d) Personal choice of hand use

5. In the historical context, what negative association has been linked to left-handedness?

    a) Strength and power

    b) Superior intelligence

    c) Sinister connotations

    d) Cultural admiration

6. What does the term "neurological" pertain to in the discussion of hand preference?

    a) Genetic traits

    b) Brain and nerves

    c) Cultural norms

    d) Environmental influences

7. What is a "predisposition" in the context of hand preference?

    a) The ability to use both hands equally

    b) A tendency or inclination toward a particular behavior

    c) Passing of genetic traits

    d) A historical negative association

8. What is a "norm" regarding hand preference?

    a) A tendency or inclination toward a particular behavior

    b) A standard or pattern considered typical within a society

    c) The passing of genetic traits

    d) The ability to use both hands equally

9. What does the term "stigma" mean in the context of hand preference?

   a) A tendency or inclination toward a particular behavior

   b) Passing of genetic traits

   c) A mark of disgrace or shame associated with a characteristic

   d) The ability to use both hands equally

10. What does the term "intricate" mean in the discussion of hand preference?

   a) The passing of genetic traits

   b) Complicated, detailed, and complex in structure or design

   c) The ability to use both hands equally

   d) A standard or pattern considered typical within a society

Answers

   1. c

   2. c

   3. b

   4. a

   5. c

   6. b

   7. b

   8. b

   9. c

   10. b

Day 45: Getting Caught

Once upon a time, in a small town called Willowbrook, there was a **diligent** student named Emily. She was known for her exceptional academic performance and had always been praised for her honesty and integrity. However, as the final exams approached, Emily found herself overwhelmed with stress and anxiety. The pressure to excel in every subject had started to take a toll on her.

One day, while studying in the library, Emily noticed a fellow classmate named Alex. Alex was **notorious** for his laziness and lack of interest in academics. He always seemed to find shortcuts to avoid studying. Intrigued, Emily approached him and asked if he had any tips to cope with the mounting stress.

With a mischievous smile, Alex leaned in and whispered, "I have a secret method that guarantees success on any exam. All you need is a small cheat sheet hidden in your pencil case. No one will ever notice."

Emily hesitated at first, but the temptation of an easy solution overwhelmed her. She decided to give it a try. Late that night, she **meticulously** prepared a cheat sheet with all the answers she thought she might need.

The next day, as the exam began, Emily took a deep breath and placed the cheat sheet inside her pencil case. However, as she started to write, her heart raced, and her **conscience** weighed heavy on her. Each glance at the cheat sheet brought a pang of guilt. She knew deep down that cheating was wrong, no matter the circumstances.

Just as she was about to surrender to her guilt and put the cheat sheet away, the invigilator, Ms. Thompson, noticed a piece of paper sticking out from Emily's pencil case. Suspicion grew on her face as she approached Emily's desk. The room fell silent as all eyes turned toward her.

Ms. Thompson sternly asked, "Emily, what is that paper in your pencil case?"

Emily's face flushed with embarrassment as she realized her moment of weakness was about to be exposed. She took a deep breath, her voice trembling, and confessed, "It's a **cheat sheet**, Ms. Thompson. I made a terrible mistake."

The entire room gasped in disbelief. Ms. Thompson, disappointed but determined to teach Emily a valuable lesson, took the cheat sheet and handed it to the principal. Emily was asked to leave the examination hall, and her paper would be marked as a zero.

Feeling **humiliated**, Emily realized the consequences of her actions. She had not only let herself down but had also betrayed the trust of her teachers, classmates, and most importantly, herself. As she walked home that day, tears streaming down her face, she vowed never to compromise her integrity again.

In the days that followed, Emily faced the consequences of her decision. She retaught herself the material she had tried to cheat on, spending countless hours studying late into the night. She even sought help from her teachers to make amends and learn from her mistake.

Over time, Emily's hard work and determination paid off. Although she couldn't change her past, she used her experience to grow stronger and became an **advocate** for academic integrity. She shared her story with her classmates and stressed the importance of honesty, reminding them that true success comes from dedication and perseverance.

Vocabulary

diligent: Showing care about one's work.

notorious: Famous or well-known for something.

meticulously: Doing something carefully, paying close attention to detail.

conscience: An inner feeling or voice about what is right.

cheat sheet: A small piece of paper that helps someone cheat on an exam.

humiliated: Very embarrassed.

advocate: A person who publicly supports a cause of some kind.

Comprehension Questions

1. How are Emily and Alex different from each other?

2. Why was Emily tempted to cheat?

3. Why was Emily humiliated?

4. What is academic integrity?

Answers

1. Emily is a good student, while Alex is known for being lazy.

2. She was tempted because she was under a lot of pressure to do well in all of her classes.

3. She was humiliated because her teacher caught her cheating.

4. Academic integrity is morality, as it relates to studies (not cheating!).

Let's Talk More

1. Have you ever been tempted to cheat on something? Did you end up doing it?

2. Should punishment be lenient or harsh for something like this story?

3. Do cheaters hurt themselves? Give your opinion.

4. What would you do if you saw a classmate cheating on a test?

5. Does everyone cheat on things like taxes?

Day 46: Nice Weather and Weekend Plans

Tim and Carrie are talking about their weekend plans.

Tim: The weather looks great for the weekend. Do you have any plans?

Carrie: I'm going to get my garden ready for planting. I have **my work cut out for me**. It's so overgrown. But, it's not **set in stone**. I'll see what else comes up!

Tim: Yeah, it is that time of year, right? The days are getting longer. I'm going to **play it by ear**. Honestly, I'm pretty **burned out** and am **barely treading water**. The **fallout** from the **cost-cutting measures** has had a huge impact on me.

Carrie: Sorry to hear that. Is there anything I can do to help?

Tim: Nah, it's okay. Gotta **bring home the bacon**, right? It's not all **doom and gloom**. I may go to a movie or something.

Carrie: You **got hit hard by** that. Don't you want to **throw in the towel?**

Vocabulary

my work cut out for me: A big or difficult job to do.

set in stone: Decided 100%.

burned out: Tired, stressed and overworked.

treading water: Barely keeping up with work or school.

fallout: Negative consequences.

cost-cutting measures: Something done to save money.

bring home the bacon: Make money with a job.

doom and gloom: Only bad things.

got hit hard by: To be badly affected by something.

throw in the towel: To quit or give up.

Practice

1. I'm barely _____ at my new job and am worried that I'll get fired.

2. We're not the only ones who _____ by Covid-19.

3. I hate my job but someone has to _____.

4. It's not all _____. He did get a B+ in English.

5. I have _____ with this new team.

6. I quit that job because I was so _____.

7. The _____ went too far I think. We're so understaffed now.

8. Nobody anticipated this would be the _____ from that decision.

9. Someone has to get fired but nothing is _____.

10. I'm ready to _____ on that project! It's brought me nothing but grief.

Answers

1. treading water

2. got hit hard by

3. bring home the bacon

4. doom and gloom

5. my work cut out for me

6. burned out

7. cost-cutting measures

8. fallout

9. set in stone

10. throw in the towel

Day 47: Opening Night

Sid and Manny are talking about the new James Bond movie.

Sid: Are you going to watch that new James Bond movie? It **comes out** on the 22nd.

Manny: Oh yeah, I never miss an **opening night** for a Bond movie. I've seen the **movie trailer** at least 10 times now. It's going to be a huge **box office hit**.

Sid: I heard that Tom Cruise has a **supporting role** and that Brad Pitt plays the **main character**. That's pretty impressive.

Manny: For sure. What about you? Will you be there on opening night?

Sid: Not in the **movie theater** but I'll watch it when I can **download it for free**!

Vocabulary

comes out: Begins.

opening night: The first night of something (movie, play, etc.)

movie trailer: A short teaser to entice you to watch the full movie.

box office hit: A movie that makes lots of money.

supporting role: Not the lead actor/actress.

main character: The leading person in a book/movie/TV show, etc.

movie theater: Place you watch movies.

download it for free: Getting a movie/TV show/software/music from the Internet and not paying for it.

Practice

1. Why pay for it when you can _____?

2. Do you know when that _____ on Netflix?

3. Do you think our local _____ will survive Covid-19?

4. Have you seen the _____ for that one yet?

5. The _____ in that book was so complex.

6. She was amazing in that _____. She stole the show.

7. I love to go to a play's _____. There's a different kind of buzz.

8. What's going to be the _____ of the year?

Answers

1. download it for free

2. comes out

3. movie theater

4. movie trailer

5. main character

6. supporting role

7. opening night

8. box office hit

Day 48: Transform

Ethan is talking with Kara about her garden.

Ethan: What are you up to this weekend?

Kara: I'm going to work on my garden. I want to **transform** it from a patch of mud to something beautiful! I'm going to **purchase** a water fountain and **feature** that in the middle. I'll have to **remove** a huge patch of weeds first though.

Ethan: That sounds quite **ambitious**. I'm such a **novice** gardener. What's the opposite of a green thumb?

Kara: You can learn! It's not an **innate** thing. Why don't you come over and help me?

Ethan: Oh, that sounds interesting actually. As long as I can bring over my outdoor chairs. Will you help me **refurbish** them?

Kara: Sure, we can work on that too.

Vocabulary

transform: Change.

purchase: Buy.

feature: Make central; highlight.

remove: Take away.

ambitious: Describes someone who is motivated.

novice: Describes someone who is a beginner.

innate: Natural; born with someone.

refurbish: Renovate; make better.

Practice

1. Do you really think we can _____ this room in a weekend? It might be too _____.

2. He had _____ musical ability, even when we was a very small child.

3. Our next big _____ will be a new car.

4. Why don't we _____ product ABC during the presentation?

5. I want to _____ this old dresser. I don't think it'll be that difficult.

6. I play tennis, but I'm a _____.

7. If we _____ this old couch, you'll have a lot more space for yoga.

Answers

1. transform, ambitious

2. innate

3. purchase

4. feature

5. refurbish

6. novice

7. remove

Day 49: The Dog and His Reflection

In a small village, there lived a friendly dog named Max. Max was known for his shiny coat and **wagging** tail. One day, as Max was strolling near a sparkling pond, he noticed something peculiar - another dog just like him! Max barked at the other dog, and it barked back. He wagged his tail, and the other dog did the same.

Deciding to investigate further, Max jumped into the **pond**, creating ripples in the water. To his surprise, the other dog did the same. Max spun around in excitement, and again, the dog in the water copied his every move.

Max thought he had found the most wonderful playmate. He **barked** louder, wagged his tail faster, and even did a little dance. Each time, the dog in the water mimicked him perfectly.

Feeling proud of his new friend, Max continued his antics until he noticed something strange. When he dropped a stick into the water, the other dog didn't drop one back. Instead, the stick disappeared into the depths of the pond. Confused, Max realized that the other dog wasn't a real friend but just his own **reflection** in the water. He felt a bit silly but also learned an important lesson.

From that day on, whenever Max saw his reflection, he remembered not to be fooled by appearances. He knew that real friends were the ones who shared sticks and played together in the sunshine.

The Moral

The moral of the story is to be careful not to be fooled by appearances. It's important to distinguish between what's real and what's just a reflection. True friends are the ones who share and play together, not just those who mimic our actions.

Vocabulary

pond: A small body of water (smaller than a lake).

wagging: Moving a tail of an animal around quickly.

reflection: An image seen on a shiny surface like water or a mirror.

barked: Made a sound (dog).

Comprehension Questions

1. What did Max notice near the pond one sunny day?
2. Why did Max think he found a new friend?
3. What did Max realize when he dropped a stick into the water?
4. What lesson did Max learn from the experience?
5. How did Max feel when he discovered the truth about the water dog?

Answers

1. Max noticed another dog that looked just like him, but in the water.
2. Max thought he found a new friend because the other dog in the water mimicked his actions and played with him.
3. Max realized that the other dog in the water wasn't a real friend because it didn't give the stick back.
4. Max learned not to be fooled by appearances and to look for real friends who share and play together.
5. Max felt a bit silly when he realized the water dog was just his reflection, not a real friend.

Day 50: Save me a Seat

Jerry and Sid are talking about coming late to class.

Jerry: Hey Sid, can you **save me a seat** in class? I'm going to **come late**.

Sid: **Take your time**. I'll even **take notes** for you. But, why are you always late?

Jerry: You know the cute girls always catch my eye and then I have to stop and talk. But, **keep up the good work** my friend. I love that you always **pay attention** in class.

Sid: Will you ever **evolve** into a responsible student?! Anyway, we should **have lunch** after class. What do you think?

Jerry: Sounds great. **In light of** what a good friend you are, it's **my treat**.

Vocabulary

save me a seat: Hold a chair or spot for someone at an event, meeting, class, etc.

come late: Show up not on time.

take your time: Don't worry about hurrying.

take notes: Write down briefly what is being heard.

keep up the good work: Continue doing the good things you're doing.

pay attention: Look closely; focus.

have lunch: Eat lunch together.

evolve: Develop or improve to a better state; change for the better.

in light of: Taking into consideration.

my treat: I'll pay.

Practice

1. Do you want to _____ next Friday?

2. Please _____! You'll need to know this for your test next week.

3. Our company needs to _____ if we want to survive.

4. If you _____ to Dr. Kim's class, you have to sit in the front row.

5. Jeremy, _____. You did so well on your exam.

6. _____ this new information, we should have another meeting to discuss things.

7. Don't worry about the prices. It's _____.

8. Please _____. I'm going to be a little bit late getting there.

9. Please _____ for this meeting, okay?

10. _____ doing this test. You have two hours to do it. It's more than enough.

Answers

1. have lunch

2. pay attention

3. evolve

4. come late

5. keep up the good work

6. in light of

7. my treat

8. save me a seat

9. take notes

10. take your time

Day 51: The Enigma of Dinosaur Extinction

The extinction of dinosaurs, marking the end of the Mesozoic Era about 66 million years ago, stands as a **captivating** and transformative event in Earth's history. Unraveling the mysteries surrounding this mass extinction involves exploring the interplay of cosmic and terrestrial factors that forever **altered** the planet's ecosystems.

Asteroid Impact Hypothesis: Unveiling Catastrophe

At the **heart** of the extinction **narrative** lies the asteroid impact hypothesis, suggesting a colossal asteroid struck near the Yucatan Peninsula, creating the Chicxulub crater and triggering a chain of catastrophic events. The immediate aftermath included wildfires, earthquakes, and a mega-tsunami. The ensuing "impact winter," caused by debris in the atmosphere, led to a dramatic reduction in sunlight, severely disrupting ecosystems by **hampering** photosynthesis.

Volcanic Activity: The Earth's Fury Unleashed

In tandem with the asteroid impact, extensive volcanic activity in the Deccan Traps of India added to the environmental turmoil. The eruption of lava released significant amounts of greenhouse gases, including carbon dioxide and sulfur dioxide, potentially contributing to climate change, altered weather patterns, and further stressing ecosystems already reeling from the asteroid impact.

Consequences on Life: The Demise and the Rise

The combined environmental upheaval resulted in profound consequences for life on Earth. Iconic species like Tyrannosaurus rex and Triceratops faced extinction, along with marine reptiles, ammonites, and various plant species. Simultaneously, the extinction event provided opportunities for mammals, previously overshadowed by dinosaurs, to flourish. The rise of mammals into diverse ecological roles eventually set the stage for the emergence of modern mammals, including humans.

Confirmation through Geological Clues

The asteroid impact hypothesis finds crucial support in geological evidence. The discovery of an iridium-rich sediment layer, shocked quartz, and microtektites in the geologic record aligns with the aftermath of an extraterrestrial impact. Additionally, geological studies of the Deccan Traps lava flows help establish the timing of volcanic activity in relation to the mass extinction event.

Ongoing Exploration: Refining the Extinction Story

While the asteroid impact hypothesis is widely accepted, ongoing research continues to refine our understanding of the specific sequence of events and the relative importance of each contributing factor. Advances in geology, paleontology, and astrobiology contribute to a more comprehensive narrative of this pivotal moment in Earth's history.

Conclusion

In conclusion, the extinction of dinosaurs remains a captivating tale, woven with cosmic collisions, volcanic fury, and the resilience of life. The legacy of this mass extinction event endures in the fossil record, offering valuable insights into the interconnected web of Earth's history and the ever-evolving drama of life on our planet.

Vocabulary

extinction: The complete disappearance of a species or group of organisms from Earth.

Mesozoic era: The geological era that spans from approximately 252 to 66 million years ago, characterized by the dominance of dinosaurs and the evolution of various plant and animal groups.

cataclysmic: Involving or causing a sudden and violent upheaval, often with widespread and severe consequences.

interplay: The dynamic interaction or reciprocal influence of different elements.

148

photosynthesis: The process by which green plants and some other organisms convert light energy into chemical energy, producing oxygen and carbohydrates from carbon dioxide and water.

Iridium: A dense, corrosion-resistant metal that is rare on Earth's surface but often associated with extraterrestrial objects such as asteroids.

tsunami: A series of ocean waves with extremely long wavelengths and high energy, typically caused by underwater disturbances such as earthquakes or asteroid impacts.

greenhouse gases: Gases in the Earth's atmosphere, such as carbon dioxide and methane, that trap heat and contribute to the greenhouse effect, leading to an increase in global temperatures.

ecological niches: The role or function of an organism or species within an ecosystem, including how it obtains and utilizes resources and interacts with other organisms.

Paleontology: The scientific study of the history of life on Earth through the examination of plant and animal fossils.

Vocabulary Challenge

1. Captivating, in the first paragraph is closest in meaning to:

    a) attracting and holding interest

    b) key

    c) unknown

    d) holding hostage

2. Altered, in the first paragraph is closest in meaning to:

   a) tailored

   b) made structural changes to a building

   c) had a small impact

   d) changed

3. Heart, in the second paragraph is closest in meaning to:

   a) a body part

   b) a shape

   c) part of something

   d) the central part of something

4. Narrative, in the second paragraph is most closely related to:

   a) distinct from dialogue

   b) story

   c) a kind of poem

   d) part of a movie

5. Hampering, in the second paragraph is most closely related to:

   a) slowing down

   b) going at the same speed

   c) stopping completely

   d) speeding up

Answers

   1. a

   2. d

   3. d

   4. b

   5. a

Comprehension Questions

1. What is the Mesozoic Era known for?

   a) Ice ages

   b) Dominance of dinosaurs

   c) Rise of mammals

   d) Human civilization

2. What process involves converting light energy into chemical energy, producing oxygen and carbohydrates?

   a) Respiration

   b) Photosynthesis

   c) Decomposition

   d) Fermentation

3. What metal is often associated with extraterrestrial objects such as asteroids and is crucial evidence supporting the asteroid impact hypothesis?

   a) Iron

   b) Iridium

   c) Gold

   d) Copper

4. Which geological era spans from approximately 252 to 66 million years ago and is characterized by the dominance of dinosaurs?

   a) Paleozoic Era

   b) Cenozoic Era

   c) Mesozoic Era

   d) Precambrian Era

5. What term describes the interaction or reciprocal influence of different elements, such as factors contributing to the extinction of dinosaurs?

a) Cataclysmic

b) Mesozoic

c) Interplay

d) Extinction

6. Which natural disaster, often triggered by underwater disturbances, involves a series of ocean waves with long wavelengths and high energy?

a) Hurricane

b) Earthquake

c) Tsunami

d) Tornado

7. What is the process by which organisms break down organic matter, returning essential nutrients to the ecosystem?

a) Photosynthesis

b) Decomposition

c) Fermentation

d) Respiration

8. What gases, including carbon dioxide and methane, contribute to the greenhouse effect and global warming?

a) Nitrogen and oxygen

b) Hydrogen and helium

c) Greenhouse gases

d) Sulfur dioxide and nitrogen oxides

9. What term describes the complete disappearance of a species or group of organisms from Earth?

    a) Evolution

    b) Extinction

    c) Adaptation

    d) Speciation

10. What scientific field focuses on the study of the history of life on Earth through the examination of plant and animal fossils?

    a) Geology

    b) Biology

    c) Paleontology

    d) Archaeology

Answers

1. b
2. b
3. b
4. c
5. c
6. c
7. b
8. c
9. b
10. c

Day 52: Get a Job

Tony is sharing some bad news with Athena.

Tony: Some **bad news**. I **was fired** from my job last month.

Athena: Seriously? What happened?

Tony: Well, there was a **heavy workload** and they wanted us to **work overtime** but for just the regular **pay rate**. That's ridiculous for a **minimum wage** job.

Athena: You shouldn't have to do overtime without pay. Are you okay for money?

Tony: Yes, I have an **emergency fund** that can cover my **living expenses** for a few months. I also have a **job interview** lined up next week for a **well-paid job**.

Vocabulary

bad news: Not good news.

was fired: Lost a job, usually due to poor performance.

heavy workload: Very busy at work or school, often more than someone can handle.

work overtime: Work beyond normal work hours.

pay rate: How much you get paid for a job, usually per hour (for example $10/hour).

minimum wage: The minimum amount of money a job can legally pay (set by the government).

emergency fund: Money stored away to use in case of an emergency.

living expenses: How much it costs to live each month for housing, car, food, etc.

job interview: An interview between an employer and a potential employee.

well-paid job: A job that pays more than usual.

Practice

1. My son just got a _____. I'm so proud of him!

2. He _____ from his last job. I don't understand why we'd want to hire him then.

3. My _____ is next Thursday at 9:30.

4. The _____ in BC is $15.25/hour.

5. I have an _____ of $10,000. It's enough for at least a few months.

6. That program has a _____ but if you finish, you're almost guaranteed to get a good job.

7. The _____ is that you're going to have to work this weekend.

8. That's a very high _____ for that kind of job, isn't it?

9. My _____ each month are around $2000.

10. I try to _____ whenever possible. I need the cash.

Answers

1. well-paid job

2. was fired

3. job interview

4. minimum wage

5. emergency fund

6. heavy workload

7. bad news

8. pay rate

9. living expenses

10. work overtime

Day 53: Learning to Play Tennis

Emily was always fascinated by sports, and she dreamt of becoming a skilled tennis player. One sunny day, as she passed by the local tennis court, she saw a group of people playing and having fun. Their energetic movements and the sound of the ball hitting the racket excited her. That's when Emily decided to **embark** on her journey to learn how to play tennis.

With **determination** in her heart, Emily approached the coach at the tennis court, Mr. Johnson. She shyly asked him if he would be willing to teach her how to play tennis. Mr. Johnson was delighted to see Emily's enthusiasm and agreed to be her coach.

They started their first lesson by teaching Emily the basic rules of tennis. Mr. Johnson explained that the **objective** was to hit the ball over the net and inside the boundary lines. He showed her the proper grip and how to position her feet.

Emily practiced diligently, hitting the ball back and forth with Mr. Johnson. At first, she struggled to control the racket and make accurate shots. But she didn't give up. She knew that learning something new takes time and patience.

As weeks turned into months, Emily's skills improved. She began to understand the different types of shots like forehand, backhand, and volley. She learned how to serve the ball and how to move swiftly around the court. Mr. Johnson encouraged her every step of the way, praising her effort and progress.

Emily also started participating in friendly matches with other beginners. She faced some tough opponents, but she never let failure discourage her. Instead, she saw each match as an opportunity to learn and grow. She analyzed her mistakes and worked on improving her weaknesses.

Over time, Emily's hard work paid off. She became more confident on the tennis court, winning matches against players who were once better than her. Her dedication and passion for the game **propelled** her forward.

One day, Emily received an invitation to compete in a local tennis tournament. Excited and nervous, she accepted the challenge. The tournament was a big test of her skills and mental strength. Emily faced strong opponents, but she played with determination and a smile on her face. She put all her training and knowledge into practice.

To her surprise, Emily reached the final match. It was a tough battle, but Emily fought hard and stayed focused. Finally, the moment arrived. Emily won the final point, and the crowd **erupted** in applause. She couldn't believe it—she had won the tournament! It was a remarkable achievement for someone who had started as a beginner not too long ago.

Emily's journey to learn tennis taught her valuable lessons about **perseverance**, dedication, and the joy of pursuing one's passion. She realized that success is not measured by the trophies won but by the growth and progress made along the way.

From that day forward, Emily continued to play tennis, always striving to improve and reach new heights. She became an inspiration to other aspiring tennis players, showing them that with determination and hard work, dreams can come true.

Vocabulary

embark: Begin something.

determination: A strong intention to do something.

objective: Aim or goal.

propelled: Pushed forward.

erupted: Explode with noise (can also refer to a volcano).

perseverance: Doing something despite difficulty.

Comprehension Questions

1. Did Emily like sports?
2. Who is Mr. Johnson?
3. How good of a student of tennis was Emily?
4. What is Emily's attitude towards losing a tennis match?
5. Was it surprising that Emily won the tournament she entered?

Answers

1. Yes, she enjoyed lots of sports.

2. Mr. Johnson is Emily's tennis coach.

3. She was an excellent student of tennis. She worked very hard to improve her skills.

4. She has a good attitude towards losing. She just sees it as an opportunity to learn from her mistakes.

5. Yes, it was quite surprising since it was her first one.

Let's Talk More

1. Have you ever worked hard to learn something new? What was it?

2. How do you view failure?

3. When learning something new, what are some important qualities to have if you want to eventually be very good at it?

4. Have you ever played tennis or another racquet sport? Did you enjoy it?

5. Is winning, or the journey along the way most important to you in competitive activities that you do?

Day 54: Beef Up

Tim and Nathan are talking about cybersecurity at their company.

Tim: I think we need to **beef up** our cybersecurity. We're starting to **fall behind,** and I'm nervous we might **end up** getting hacked.

Nathan: I agree. It's time to **break out** all the tools. I'd rather do some prevention now if it means we don't have to **fight back** against some unknown enemy later.

Tim: I agree. Let's **get it over with**. We have to do it at some point and better late than never.

Nathan: For sure. But, we can't get **carried away** with it. We still have to **stay within** the budget. Let's **hit up** Tony and see what he thinks about this. He's the head of security here.

Vocabulary

beef up: Increase.

fall behind: Not keep up with others.

end up: To be in a place that was not planned for in the end.

break out: Deploy or start to use something.

fight back: Counterattack in a fight or battle.

get it over with: Do something that you don't want to do.

carried away: Do something to an excessive degree.

stay within: Not go over budget or time; not exceed some limit.

hit up: Ask someone for something, usually a favour.

Practice

1. We need to _____ the schedule time for this meeting. I have a dentist appointment after it.

2. I don't want to _____ being stuck next to him at lunch.

3. We're starting to _____ on this project. Let's stay late tonight and tomorrow and try to get back on track.

4. Let's _____ against Tim about this decision. It's clearly the wrong one for our company.

5. My kids always get _____ with games and never clean up!

6. Let's _____ your parents and see if they'll take us out for dinner tonight.

7. Let's _____ that wine you made. I think it's ready.

8. Cleaning the garage this weekend? I don't want to but let's _____.

9. Let's _____ our home security system. There have been a lot of break-ins recently.

Answers

1. stay within

2. end up

3. fall behind

4. fight back

5. carried away

6. hit up

7. break out

8. get it over with

9. beef up

Day 55: Breaking Out in a Cold Sweat

Tom is a mature student who is talking to Jackie about studying for an exam.

Tom: I've been **breaking out in a cold sweat** a lot lately. I'm **a bundle of nerves**. I'm not used to having to study so much.

Jackie: What are you studying for?

Tom: I have to pass this exam for work and I'll lose my job if I don't. I'm maybe **making a mountain of a molehill** but I can't help being nervous about it. It's been so long since I've had to take a test.

Jackie: It's **like riding a bike**. You'll get back into it once you start. **Go with the flow.**

Tom: Do you have any **study tips**?

Jackie: My best advice is to study a little bit every day instead of pulling all-nighters or **cramming**. That doesn't work. Give yourself time to **chew it over**.

Vocabulary

breaking out in a cold sweat: To be afraid or nervous about something.

a bundle of nerves: Describes someone who is very nervous or worried about something.

making a mountain out of a molehill: To make something into a bigger deal than it is. For example, someone who loses sleep over a small problem.

like riding a bike: Something that you always remember how to do, even with a large break in between.

go with the flow: To relax and go along with whatever happens.

study tips: Ideas for how to study more effectively.

cramming: Trying to learn everything for a test at the last minute.

chew it over: In this case, means taking time and not rushing when considering the test material.

Practice

1. You'll get the hang of it. It's _____.

2. This final exam has me _____. I'm so worried about it.

3. I think you need to _____ with this school project. It sounds like you're taking it way more seriously than the other people in your group.

4. I'll have to _____ for a for a few days. Can I let you know next week?

5. I don't think that _____ is a very effective study method.

6. You're _____ right now. Is anything wrong?

7. One of the best _____ is to do it for one hour and then take a 10-minute break.

8. I think you're _____. It's not a big deal!

Answers

1. like riding a bike

2. breaking out in a cold sweat

3. go with the flow

4. chew it over

5. cramming

6. a bundle of nerves

7. study tips

8. making a mountain out of a molehill

162

Day 56: An Introduction to Economics

Economics serves as a comprehensive social science that **probes** the intricate ways in which individuals, businesses, and societies manage and allocate resources to fulfill their **insatiable** wants and needs. This field extends its reach from the intricacies of personal decision-making to the broader spectrum of global economic trends.

The Foundation: Scarcity and Decision-Making

At the heart of economic principles lies the concept of scarcity. This arises due to the inherent limitation of resources such as time, money, and natural assets, **juxtaposed** against the boundless human desires. Consequently, individuals, businesses, and governments must navigate the challenge of making choices and trade-offs to **optimize** resource allocation and achieve their respective objectives.

Microeconomics: Decoding Individual Behavior

Microeconomics, as a foundational **pillar**, concentrates on the behavior of discrete entities such as households, firms, and markets. This branch of economics scrutinizes the decision-making processes of consumers and firms, unraveling the complexities of choices, production, and pricing strategies. Furthermore, microeconomics delves into the nuances of market structures, including perfect competition, monopoly, and oligopoly, which shape the dynamics of supply and demand.

Macroeconomics: A Holistic Perspective

Taking a panoramic view, macroeconomics focuses on the comprehensive performance of an entire economy. Key indicators such as inflation, unemployment, economic growth, and government policies fall under its scrutiny. Macroeconomists seek to comprehend the factors influencing these broad-scale indicators and devise strategies to foster stability and enhancement on a national or global economic scale.

The Market Forces: Supply and Demand Dynamics

Central to economic discourse is the elemental interplay between supply and demand. These twin forces dictate prices and quantities within markets. When demand surpasses supply, prices ascend, incentivizing producers to increase output. Conversely, when supply outstrips demand, prices decline, prompting producers to scale back production. This dynamic equilibrium serves as a fundamental driver of economic transactions.

Government's Role: Policies and Interventions

Beyond market forces, economists investigate the role of governments in shaping economic outcomes. Through policies such as taxation, subsidies, and regulations, governments intervene to address market failures, foster fair competition, and promote societal well-being. Striking the delicate balance between market autonomy and government intervention is a perennial subject of debate in economic theory and policy discussions.

Economic Systems: Capitalism, Socialism, and Beyond

Economic systems, ranging from capitalism to socialism, exert a profound influence on the economic landscape. Capitalist economies emphasize private ownership and free markets, while socialist economies advocate for collective or government ownership and control. The study of economics unveils the strengths and weaknesses inherent in each system, contributing to ongoing discussions about the optimal economic structure.

Conclusion: Empowering Informed Decision-Making

In conclusion, economics provides a robust framework for deciphering the multifaceted decisions and interactions that propel our global society. Equipping individuals with tools to analyze supply and demand, decipher market structures, comprehend government policies, and assess economic systems, the study of economics fosters informed decision-making across personal, business, and policy realms. As we explore the intricate web of economic forces, we gain valuable insights into the mechanisms shaping our world and steering the well-being of individuals and societies.

Vocabulary

scarcity: The fundamental economic concept that refers to the limited availability of resources in comparison to the unlimited human wants and needs.

microeconomics: The branch of economics that focuses on the behaviors and decisions of individual entities such as households, businesses, and markets.

macroeconomics: The study of the overall performance and behavior of an entire economy, examining indicators like inflation, unemployment, and economic growth.

supply and demand: The fundamental forces driving market dynamics, where supply represents the quantity of a good or service available, and demand is the quantity buyers are willing to purchase at a given price.

government intervention: Actions taken by the government in the economy, such as regulations, subsidies, and taxes, to address market failures or promote certain outcomes.

market structures: The different organizational arrangements of markets, including perfect competition, monopoly, and oligopoly, influencing pricing and competition.

inflation: A sustained increase in the general price level of goods and services in an economy, resulting in a decrease in the purchasing power of a currency.

unemployment: The condition where individuals who are willing and able to work are unable to find employment.

capitalism: An economic system characterized by private ownership of resources and the means of production, with a focus on free-market competition.

socialism: An economic system advocating for collective or government ownership and control of the means of production, aiming for more equitable distribution of wealth and resources.

Vocabulary Challenge

1. Probes, in the first paragraph is most closely related to:

    a) space exploration

    b) seeks to uncover information

    c) done in surgery

    d) tries

2. insatiable, in the first paragraph is most closely related to:

    a) thirsty

    b) without end

    c) unable to do something

    d) impossible to satisfy

3. juxtaposed, in the second paragraph is most closely related to:

    a) a visual effect

    b) something social scientists do

    c) related to comparing things

    d) an economic term

4. Optimize, in the second paragraph is most closely related to:

    a) make the best use of something

    b) to begin something

    c) related to sight

    d) to finish something

5. Pillar, in the third paragraph is most closely related to:

a) a strong piece of wood or steel

b) medication

c) something that provides support

d) a support structure for a building

Answers

1. b

2. d

3. c

4. a

5. c

Multiple Choice Questions

1. What is the fundamental economic concept that arises due to the limited availability of resources compared to unlimited human wants and needs?

a. Abundance

b. Wealth

c. Scarcity

d. Surplus

2. Which branch of economics focuses on the behaviors and decisions of individual entities such as households, businesses, and markets?

a. Macroeconomics

b. Microeconomics

c. Econometrics

d. Behavioral Economics

3. What term describes the forces that determine prices and quantities in markets, where supply represents availability and demand reflects consumer desire?

a. Competition

b. Equilibrium

c. Monopoly

d. Inflation

4. In economics, what does the term "inflation" refer to?

a. Decrease in the money supply

b. Rise in the general price level

c. Increase in unemployment

d. Contraction of the economy

5. What does the government often use to address market failures and promote specific economic outcomes?

a. Taxes

b. Subsidies

c. Regulations

d. All of the above

6. Which economic system is characterized by private ownership of resources and a focus on free-market competition?

a. Socialism

b. Capitalism

c. Communism

d. Fascism

7. What is the term for the condition where individuals who are willing and able to work cannot find employment?

    a. Underemployment

    b. Disemployment

    c. Unemployment

    d. Overemployment

8. Which economic indicator is concerned with the overall performance and behavior of an entire economy?

    a. Microeconomic indicators

    b. Inflation rate

    c. Unemployment rate

    d. Macroeconomic indicators

9. What is the economic term for actions taken by the government in the market, such as setting prices or limiting competition?

    a. Market forces

    b. Government intervention

    c. Price control

    d. Market equilibrium

10. What is the study of different organizational arrangements of markets, including perfect competition, monopoly, and oligopoly?

    a. Market segmentation

    b. Market structures

    c. Market equilibrium

    d. Market dynamics

Answers

1. c
2. b
3. b
4. b
5. d
6. b
7. c
8. d
9. b
10. b

Day 57: At a Loss

Ted is trying to buy a used laptop from a shopkeeper.

Shopkeeper: Can I help you with something? We have lots of new arrivals **for sale**.

Ted: I'm interested in this laptop, but why is it so expensive? It's used, right?

Shopkeeper: Well, used laptops are **in high demand.** The ones you see will all be sold within a week. They're of the highest quality and we've checked them for viruses and wiped them clean.

Ted: I'm willing to pay **at most** $800 for it.

Shopkeeper: I can't sell you something **at a loss**! It just doesn't make sense.

Ted: Under no circumstances will I pay more than $800, and that's the computer I want.

Shopkeeper: I can't do it. **By all means**, feel free to take your business elsewhere.

Vocabulary

for sale: Available to buy.

in high demand: Lots of people want it.

at most: The maximum.

at a loss: To lose money on a deal.

under no circumstances: Never, no matter what happens.

by all means: Of course; certainly.

Practice

1. I'm hoping to pay _____ $500 for that.

2. _____ will I become a doctor, even though my parents want me to.

3. _____, check our competitors and see what they're charging.

4. The new iPhone is _____.

5. When we got divorced, we were forced to sell our house _____.

Answers

1. at most

2. under no circumstances

3. by all means

4. in high demand

5. at a loss

Day 58: Online Dating

Jen and Tina are talking about online dating.

Jen: Hey, so what's new with you **these days**?

Tina: Oh, not much. But I did start doing **online dating**.

Jen: Nice! How's that going?

Tina: It's like finding a **needle in a haystack**. I mean, they don't have to look like **movie stars** but I'm so tired of guys with **facial hair**—**shaggy beards** and **bushy eyebrows**. Gross.

Jen: So what are you looking for?

Tina: Nothing complicated. Someone with an **athletic build**, **outgoing personality**, and a **good sense of humour**. Shouldn't be too difficult, right?

Vocabulary

these days: Lately; recently.

online dating: Finding a love match through the Internet.

needle in a haystack: Describes something that is difficult to find.

movie stars: Famous actors or actresses.

facial hair: Beard or mustache.

shaggy beards: Beards that are not well-groomed.

bushy eyebrows: Big eyebrows that are not well-groomed.

athletic build: Describes someone in good shape who exercises a lot.

outgoing personality: Describes someone who likes being around people.

good sense of humor: Describes someone who likes to laugh and tell jokes.

Practice

1. What have you been up to _____?

2. How did he get such an _____? He must be working out a lot.

3. Guys with _____ are all the rage lately.

4. Finding my keys in the morning is like finding a _____.

5. I love that my co-worker has such a _____. I'm always laughing.

6. Who are your favourite _____?

7. I'm thinking about growing out my _____. What do you think?

8. I hate my _____. It's so much work to keep them trimmed.

9. I'm looking for someone with an _____ because I'm kind of shy.

10. I know that you don't want to but I think you'd have good luck with _____.

Answers

1. these days

2. athletic build

3. shaggy beards

4. needle in a haystack

5. good sense of humour

6. movie stars

7. facial hair

8. bushy eyebrows

9. outgoing personality

10. online dating

174

Day 59: Break a Leg

Linda is talking to Jerry about a play that she'll be in next month.

Jerry: Hey, I heard **through the grapevine** that you're going to be in a play next month.

Linda: It's true. I must admit! I had to **blow off some steam** from work and escaping into my character is a great way to do that.

Jerry: You're really **taking the bull by the horns** lately! Can I come watch?

Linda: Sure, **knock yourself out**! It's a little bit **amateur hour** but **on the upside**, the tickets are cheap!

Jerry: Okay, I'll come for sure. I can't forget to tell you to **break a leg** though!

Vocabulary

break a leg: To wish someone good luck, usually before performing or going on stage.

blow off some steam: Doing something to get rid of stress. For example, having a few drinks after a difficult work project.

knock yourself out: To try hard to do something. Often something that others think is a waste of time.

taking the bull by the horns: Doing something bravely and decisively.

through the grapevine: To spread information informally. Often related to gossip.

amateur hour: Not professional.

on the upside: Something positive in a generally negative situation.

Practice

1. I heard _____ that Tom and Monica broke up.

2. You want to do that for me? _____.

3. I starting playing soccer to _____ from my terrible job.

4. Well, _____, this job has better hours.

5. Good luck and _____.

6. It was hard to watch that presentation. Talk about _____.

7. I'm _____ at work lately and it's going well!

Answers

1. through the grapevine

2. Knock yourself out

3. blow off some steam

4. on the upside

5. break a leg

6. amateur hour

7. taking the bull by the horns

Day 60: A Bundle of Sticks

Once upon a time in a small village, there lived a family of five **siblings**. They were always **arguing** and fighting, and their parents worried about the constant discord. To teach them a valuable lesson, their wise grandmother decided to share the fable of the **Bundle** of Sticks.

One day, Grandma gathered the siblings and handed each of them a single stick. She asked them to break it, and each sibling easily snapped their stick in two. Next, Grandma handed each sibling a bundle of five sticks tied together. She challenged them to break the bundle. No matter how hard they tried, none of the siblings could break the bundle of sticks.

Grandma smiled and said, "You see, my dear ones, individually, you are like those single sticks—fragile and easily broken. But together, as a united bundle, you are strong and unbreakable." The siblings looked at each other, realizing the wisdom in Grandma's words. From that day on, they decided to stick together, supporting and helping each other through thick and thin.

The village noticed the positive change in the siblings, and their **newfound** unity brought peace and happiness to their home. The lesson of the Bundle of Sticks stayed with them throughout their lives, reminding them that strength comes from unity and cooperation. And so, the once-fighting siblings learned the power of togetherness, creating a strong **bond** that lasted a lifetime.

The moral of the story is that **unity** is strength. Just like a bundle of sticks is harder to break than a single stick, people working together can overcome challenges more easily.

The Moral

The moral of the story is that when people work together and support each other, they become stronger. Like a bunch of sticks tied together is harder to break than a single stick, unity and cooperation help us face challenges and difficulties in life.

Vocabulary

siblings: 2 or more children sharing a mother and/or father.

bundle: A collection of things wrapped together.

arguing: Expressing opinions in an angry way.

newfound: Recently discovered.

unity: The state of being joined, or of having the same opinion.

bond: A relationship between people or grounds.

Comprehension Questions

1. What was the problem with the five brothers and sisters in the story?
2. What did Grandma give each sibling to break?
3. Could the siblings easily break the single sticks?
4. What did Grandma give them next, and could they break it?
5. What did the siblings learn from this experience?

Answers

1. They always fought with each other.
2. Grandma gave each sibling a single stick.
3. Yes, they could easily break the single sticks.
4. Grandma gave them a bundle of sticks tied together, and they couldn't break it.
5. They learned that when they stay together and support each other, they are stronger, just like a bundle of sticks is harder to break than a single stick.

Day 61: In the Pipeline

A student is commenting on climate change in a class.

I think that all our discussion about climate change **overlooks** one important thing—what we eat. **Cattle** production on **factory farms** releases a massive amount of **methane gas** into the atmosphere, not to mention polluting the local water sources. This is important because it's something that individuals can have an impact on and it's time to **come to grips with** this. We need to eat less meat!

The good news is that there is a shift happening in consumer awareness. More and more plant-based meats are **in the pipeline** and they are becoming increasingly popular with consumers. These new kinds of "meat" have the potential to **transform** the way we eat. I'm **under no illusion** that we'll suddenly have more Vegans because people are worried about climate change. However, plant-based meats **have a lot of potential** if two or three times a week, people choose it instead of beef, pork, or chicken. People would be healthier too!

Vocabulary

overlooks: Fails to notice something.

cattle: A name for cows (more than 1 of them).

factory farms: Large farms that operate on a huge scale.

methane gas: A kind of gas that's released by cows as they digest food.

come to grips with: Begin to deal with.

in the pipeline: something being developed by a person, company, government, etc. that will be available soon.

transform: Dramatic change.

under no illusion: False idea or belief.

have a lot of potential: Has the ability to change into something else in the future.

Practice

1. I'm _____ that this situation will get better.

2. The _____ outside my city pollute the air, land, and water.

3. We have to _____ the fact that climate change is real.

4. _____ is a major contributor to climate change.

5. I want to _____ this piece of land into an organic farm.

6. He _____ but he needs to focus on his studies instead of playing video games.

7. We have a similar product _____. It should be available in about 6 months.

8. I'm so thankful that my teacher _____ so many errors in my writing.

9. I grew up on a farm that raised _____.

Answers

1. under no illusion

2. factory farms

3. come to grips with

4. methane gas

5. transform

6. has a lot of potential

7. in the pipeline

8. overlooks

9. cattle

Day 62: Sparks Were Flying

Richard and Candice are talking about their coworkers.

Richard: Did you hear about the fight between Tom and Carrie? **Sparks were flying**!

Candice: Oh yeah, it's **out in the open** now. I think it's **common knowledge**. I heard that Tom didn't want to **play hardball** and he was happy to let the client do things **under the table** concerning their taxes.

Richard: Yeah, and Carrie disagreed and thought it was to either get them to do things the right way or **bail on** them.

Candice: No harm done. I think it's **settled down** now. I'm happy I don't make the decisions around here!

Vocabulary

sparks were flying: There was a big conflict.

out in the open: Everyone knows about it.

common knowledge: Everyone knows about it.

play hardball: Be firm and determined to get what you want.

under the table: Something sketchy or illegal.

bail on: Quit on someone or something.

no harm done: Nothing bad happened.

settled down: Quiet, or relaxed again.

Practice

1. Let's get the kids _____ a bit before bedtime.

2. I hate doing things _____.

3. I know you want to _____ but a gentler approach will work better here.

4. Let's get this ____. I hate keeping secrets.

5. Honestly, there's _____. I don't care about that kind of thing.

6. Please don't _____ me. There's so much work to do.

7. It's _____ that Tom is terrible at his job!

8. The _____ during that meeting.

Answers

1. settled down

2. under the table

3. play hardball

4. out in the open

5. no harm done

6. bail on

7. common knowledge

8. sparks were flying

Day 63: Making Homemade Pasta

Emma loved cooking and experimenting with different recipes. One day, she decided to try her hand at making homemade **ravioli**. Little did she know, this would be a culinary adventure that would teach her valuable lessons about patience, creativity, and the joy of sharing food with loved ones.

Emma started by gathering all the ingredients she needed: all-purpose flour, eggs, salt, olive oil, ricotta cheese, Parmesan cheese, spinach, and fresh basil. She cleared the kitchen counter, washed her hands, and put on her favorite apron, ready to **embark** on her homemade ravioli journey.

First, Emma prepared the pasta dough. She poured two cups of flour onto a wooden board, making a well in the center. In the well, she cracked two eggs and added a pinch of salt. With a fork, she whisked the eggs, gradually **incorporating** the flour until it formed a sticky dough. She then sprinkled some flour on the board and kneaded the dough until it became smooth and elastic.

Covering the dough with a clean cloth, Emma let it rest for about 30 minutes. During this time, she prepared the filling by wilting the spinach in a pan with a little olive oil and garlic. Once the spinach cooled down, she mixed it with ricotta cheese, Parmesan cheese, and freshly chopped basil. The **aroma** of the herbs filled the kitchen, making Emma even more excited to taste her homemade ravioli.

After the dough had rested, Emma divided it into smaller pieces and rolled each one into thin sheets using a rolling pin. She dusted the sheets with flour to prevent sticking and then spooned small mounds of the spinach and cheese filling onto one sheet, leaving space between them. Carefully, she covered the filling with another sheet of pasta and pressed around each mound to seal the edges, using a fork to create decorative ridges.

With all the ravioli prepared, Emma brought a large pot of water to a boil, adding a pinch of salt. She gently dropped the ravioli into the bubbling water, one by one, making sure not to overcrowd the pot. As the ravioli cooked, they **floated** to the surface, indicating they were ready to be served.

Using a slotted spoon, Emma carefully lifted the cooked ravioli from the pot and placed them onto serving plates. She drizzled a simple tomato sauce over the top, garnishing with a sprinkle of Parmesan cheese and a few fresh basil leaves.

As Emma sat down to enjoy her homemade ravioli, she couldn't help but marvel at the flavors she had created from scratch. The pasta was tender, the filling bursting with vibrant colors and tastes. She savored each bite, feeling **a sense of accomplishment** and pride.

But Emma's joy didn't end there. She called her friends and invited them to join her in the kitchen. With smiles on their faces, they gathered around the table, sharing stories and laughter while enjoying the delicious homemade ravioli together. Emma realized that cooking was not only about creating tasty meals but also about bringing people closer and creating lasting memories.

Vocabulary

ravioli: A kind of pasta with a savory filling in the middle.

embark: Begin; start.

incorporating: Mixing together.

aroma: Smell.

floated: Rested or moved to the surface of a liquid without sinking.

a sense of accomplishment: A feeling or pride at having done something.

Comprehension Questions

1. Has Emma made ravioli before?
2. Do you think homemade ravioli is easy to make?
3. Once you put the filling in the dough, can you eat the ravioli?
4. What kind of sauce did she put on the ravioli?
5. Did Emma eat the ravioli by herself?

Answers

1. No, she hasn't.

2. It doesn't seem that easy to make. There are a lot of steps in the process.

3. No, you have to cook the ravioli in boiling water before you eat them.

4. She used a simple tomato sauce with a bit of fresh basil.

5. No, she invited her friends over to share the ravioli with her.

Let's Talk More

1. What do you like to cook?

2. Have you ever tried making homemade pasta? How did it go?

3. Have you ever cooked anything that took a long time and had many steps? Would you do it again?

4. Why does food bring people together?

5. What are some of the traditions surrounding food in your culture?

Day 64: Chill Out

Keith is telling Sam that he's going to leave.

Keith: Hey, I think I'm going to **bail**.

Sam: **Chill out**! You just got here. Why are you leaving?

Keith: I'm tired of playing **third wheel** with you **couch potatoes**.

Sam: Come on, stay. We'll watch **a flick** or something.

Keith: Nah, I'm going to **roll**. I want to **catch some rays** at the beach.

Sam: You're such **a pain in the neck**! Why don't we come with you though? I'm tired of sitting around too.

Vocabulary

bail: Leave; depart.

chill out: Relax.

third wheel: Describes someone who is spending time with a couple.

couch potatoes: People who aren't that active, instead preferring to sit on the couch and watch TV or play video games.

a flick: A movie.

roll: Go somewhere.

catch some rays: Go outside in the sun.

a pain in the neck: Describes someone who is annoying or bothersome.

Practice

1. My youngest is such _____.

2. Let's _____. There are some weird people here.

3. I don't mind being the _____, depending on the couple.

4. Let's _____. We need to be there in 15 minutes.

5. I want to _____ this weekend for sure.

6. Hey, _____. We don't have to be there for another hour.

7. Do you want to catch _____ this weekend?

8. My kids are basically _____ and never want to go outside.

Answers

1. a pain in the neck

2. bail

3. third wheel

4. roll

5. catch some rays

6. chill out

7. a flick

8. couch potatoes

Day 65: An Introduction to Music

Music, a universal language that transcends cultural and linguistic boundaries, has been an **integral** part of the human experience throughout history. From the rhythmic beats of ancient drums to the intricate compositions of classical symphonies and the **vibrant** melodies of contemporary genres, music reflects and shapes the diverse **tapestry** of human emotions, cultures, and societies.

The Essence of Music: A Harmonious Blend of Elements

At its core, music is an art form that involves the organized arrangement of sounds and silence. It encompasses a vast **spectrum** of styles, genres, and traditions, each offering a unique lens through which to explore and appreciate the expressive potential of sound. Whether instrumental or vocal, music has the power to **evoke** powerful emotions, tell stories, and convey complex messages without the need for words.

Rhythm: The Heartbeat of Music

One of the fundamental elements of music is rhythm, the pattern of beats and durations that provides a sense of order and structure. Rhythm is the heartbeat of music, setting the pace and creating a foundation for the other musical elements to unfold. Whether it's the steady thump of a bass drum in a rock song, the syncopated rhythms of jazz, or the intricate patterns of a tabla in Indian classical music, rhythm plays a crucial role in shaping the character and feel of a musical piece.

Melody: Crafting Memorable Tunes

Melody, another essential component of music, consists of a sequence of pitches that create a memorable and recognizable tune. Melodies can be simple or complex, ranging from the familiar tunes of nursery rhymes to the intricate and emotive lines of a violin concerto. The interplay of melodies and harmonies, the combination of different pitches played simultaneously, adds depth and richness to musical compositions.

Harmony: The Art of Sonic Texture

Harmony, the simultaneous combination of different musical notes, contributes to the texture and color of a musical piece. Whether it's the harmonious chords of a choir, the intricate interplay of instruments in an orchestra, or the dissonant tones of experimental music, harmony shapes the overall sonic landscape, creating a sense of tension or resolution.

Cultural Significance: Music as a Reflection of Society

In addition to these structural elements, music is deeply connected to cultural, social, and historical contexts. Different cultures and societies have developed their own unique musical traditions, instruments, and styles, reflecting the values, beliefs, and experiences of their communities. From the traditional folk music of a specific region to the global influence of contemporary pop and electronic music, the diversity of musical expression is a testament to the richness of human creativity.

Expressive Power: Music as Personal and Collective Expression

Music also serves as a vehicle for personal and collective expression. Artists use music to convey their emotions, tell stories, and comment on social and political issues. Whether it's the protest songs of the 1960s, the anthems that define cultural movements, or the introspective lyrics of a singer-songwriter, music has the power to inspire, provoke thought, and unite people across different backgrounds.

Evolution of Music: Technological Advancements and Global Connectivity

As technology has advanced, the ways in which we create, consume, and share music have evolved. The advent of recording technology, radio, and streaming platforms has democratized access to music, allowing artists to reach global audiences and listeners to explore a vast array of musical genres. This interconnectedness has fueled innovation and cross-cultural influences, shaping the ever-changing landscape of the music industry.

Conclusion: Music as an Essential and Enduring Human Experience

In conclusion, the world of music is a vast thing that encompasses an array of styles, traditions, and expressions. It is a powerful form of communication that has been an integral part of human history and continues to evolve in response to cultural, technological, and societal changes. Whether experienced in a concert hall or through headphones, music has the ability to inspire, move, and connect people on a profound level, making it an essential and enduring aspect of the human experience.

Vocabulary

harmony: The simultaneous combination of different musical notes to create a pleasing and balanced sound.

rhythm: The pattern of beats and durations in music, providing a sense of time and structure.

melody: A sequence of musical notes that forms a tune and is often the most memorable part of a piece.

genre: A category or style of music characterized by distinctive features, such as rock, jazz, or classical.

composition: A piece of music created by arranging and organizing musical elements like melody, harmony, and rhythm.

tempo: The speed at which a piece of music is played, influencing its mood and overall feel.

crescendo: A gradual increase in volume or intensity in a musical piece.

dynamics: The variation in loudness and intensity in music, contributing to its expressive qualities.

lyrics: The words or text of a song, often expressing emotions, stories, or messages.

instrumentation: The selection and arrangement of instruments in a musical composition or performance.

Vocabulary Challenge

1. Integral, in the first paragraph is closest in meaning to:

   a) necessary

   b) unimportant

   c) a mathematical term

   d) the most important thing

2. Vibrant, in the first paragraph is most closely related to:

   a) describes a bright color

   b) quivering

   c) dull

   d) full of energy

3. Tapestry, in the first paragraph is most closely related to:

   a) a decorative piece of cloth

   b) a collection

   c) describes a single thing

   d) a window covering

4. Spectrum, in in the second paragraph is most closely related to:

   a) various colors

   b) related to autism

   c) related to sound and particles

   d) a range

5. Evoke, in the second paragraph is most closely related to:

   a) bringing to the consciousness

   b) call on the spirits

   c) elicit a response

   d) move from one place to another

Answers

1. a

2. d

3. b

4. d

5. c

Multiple Choice Questions

1. What is the term for the simultaneous combination of different musical notes, contributing to the texture and color of a musical piece?

   a. Melody

   b. Harmony

   c. Rhythm

   d. Tempo

2. In music, what is the pattern of beats and durations that provides a sense of time and structure?

   a. Melody

   b. Harmony

   c. Rhythm

   d. Crescendo

3. Which term refers to a gradual increase in volume or intensity in a musical piece?

   a. Dynamics

   b. Crescendo

   c. Tempo

   d. Composition

192

4. What is the category or style of music characterized by distinctive features, such as rock, jazz, or classical?

    a. Melody

    b. Genre

    c. Harmony

    d. Composition

5. What is a sequence of musical notes that forms a tune and is often the most memorable part of a piece?

    a. Harmony

    b. Crescendo

    c. Melody

    d. Tempo

6. What term is used to describe the speed at which a piece of music is played, influencing its mood and overall feel?

    a. Crescendo

    b. Dynamics

    c. Tempo

    d. Genre

7. Which term refers to the variation in loudness and intensity in music, contributing to its expressive qualities?

    a. Tempo

    b. Dynamics

    c. Rhythm

    d. Composition

8. What are the words or text of a song, often expressing emotions, stories, or messages?

    a. Lyrics

    b. Harmony

    c. Instrumentation

    d. Crescendo

9. What is the term for the arrangement of instruments in a musical composition or performance?

    a. Tempo

    b. Dynamics

    c. Instrumentation

    d. Melody

10. What is a piece of music created by arranging and organizing musical elements like melody, harmony, and rhythm?

    a. Composition

    b. Genre

    c. Crescendo

    d. Lyrics

Answers

1. b
2. c
3. b
4. b
5. c
6. c
7. b
8. a
9. c
10. a

Day 66: No Pain No Gain

Jay and Lily are talking about going back to school.

Jay: I'm thinking about going back to school to study engineering! Hitting the books again. Am I crazy? I haven't been in school for years but I'm so tired of my **dead-end job**.

Lily: Well, as I like to say, "**No pain, no gain**!" If you're going to **make some bank** at a new job afterwards, then why not? You can **reinvent** yourself if you want to.

Jay: That's what I thought too. I'm going to enjoy the **calm before the storm** though. I'm going to be **as busy as a beaver** once the semester starts up in September.

Lily: Oh, you'll **weather the storm** just fine and it'll be **happily ever after** for you. You've got a **good head on your shoulders.** Let's get a beer tonight. You can tell me more about your plan.

Vocabulary

dead-end job: A job without possibility of promotion or advancement

no pain, no gain: Stress and difficulties are to be expected when doing hard work for a goal.

make some bank: To earn lots of money.

reinvent: Make something new again.

calm before the storm: A quiet period before a difficult time.

as busy as a beaver: Working a lot or very hard.

weather the storm: Make it through, or survive a difficult situation.

happily ever after: Go through the rest of your life happily.

good head on your shoulders: Has good common sense, good judgement, is practical.

Practice

1. I'm going to work up in northern Canada to _____.

2. I'm just going to enjoy the _____. Things will get crazy with final exams next month.

4. I'm trying to become an engineer. It's tough going but _____.

5. My husband works at a _____. He says the pay is terrible and they don't give raises.

6. You have a _____. You'll be fine at university.

7. Do you think that Tom and Cindy will be a _____ story?

8. It's going to take more than that to _____.

9. I want to _____ myself with a new job that allows for personal growth.

10. He's _____ with that new course he's taking.

Answers

1. make some bank

2. calm before the storm

4. no pain, no gain

5. dead-end job

6. good head on your shoulders

7. happily ever after

8. weather the storm

9. reinvent

10. as busy as a beaver

Day 67: Widespread Abuse

Tammy is talking to Cindy about a policy at her work.

Cindy: How's that new unlimited sick day policy at your work going? Did your company **proceed** with it?

Tammy: Oh, it's ridiculous. There's **widespread** abuse. Most people are taking every Friday or Monday off and getting paid for it. When they implemented it, it was **obvious** that it was never going to work.

Cindy: What happens if you get caught abusing it?

Tammy: That's the thing. Nothing. That's the **core** issue. My company is far too **lenient** on the lazy people. There was no **strategy** to encourage people to show up every day. Human resources is basically **incompetent**.

Cindy: So what's going to happen?

Tammy: Well, productivity is way down. They'll have to **suspend** it, I think.

Vocabulary

proceed: Start or continue with something.

widespread: Describes something that occurs widely, over a large area or time.

obvious: Easily understood.

core: Central, of main importance.

lenient: Not harsh; merciful.

strategy: A plan to reach a desired outcome.

incompetent: Incapable.

suspend: Stop, usually temporarily.

Practice

1. There's _____ cheating in his class. He just reads a book during tests.

2. My boss is totally _____. I'm sure she'll get fired soon.

3. We need to _____ your daughter for a week. You can't hit other kids at school.

4. My husband says I'm too _____ with the kids. He might be right.

5. Let's _____ with the sale.

6. The solution is _____ to me. We need to fire Toni.

7. What's the _____ issue here? We keep beating around the bush.

8. What's our _____ here? Should we price it high or low?

Answers

1. widespread

2. incompetent

3. suspend

4. lenient

5. proceed

6. obvious

7. core

8. strategy

Day 68: Financially Savvy

Meenu is talking to Tim about her financial situation.

Tim: What's new?

Meenu: I'm tired of **being broke** so I went to a **financial advisor**. I **make good money** but **money is tight** each month. I have no idea why.

Tim: What did they say?

Meenu: That I **waste money** like nobody's business and that I need to **make a budget** and **stick with it**.

Tim: Well, maybe it's time to get serious about **saving for retirement** at our age. I've just started **investing money in the stock market**.

Meenu: You're so **financially savvy**. I wish I knew how you did it!

Vocabulary

being broke: Not having money.

financial advisor: Someone who advises about money matters.

make good money: Gets paid a high salary.

money is tight: Short of money.

waste money: Spends money freely on frivolous things.

make a budget: Write down how much money you will spend each month.

stick with it: Not alter or change something.

saving for retirement: Saving money for after you stop working.

investing money in the stock market: Buying stocks (shares of companies).

financially savvy: Describes someone good with money.

Practice

1. They are _____ and have already paid off their mortgage.

2. I'd like to learn more about _____.

3. I hate _____.

4. Let's not _____ on eating out, okay?

5. I need to start _____ now that I'm in my thirties.

6. _____ at my house which means that we only buy used clothes.

7. I _____ but find it difficult to save. I love going out on weekends.

8. Let's _____ even though it's difficult.

9. A good _____ will help you stay on track with your goals.

10. Let's _____ together. That way, we'll both be invested in it.

Answers

1. financially savvy

2. investing money in the stock market

3. being broke

4. waste money

5. saving for retirement

6. money is tight

7. make good money

8. stick with it

9. financial advisor

10. make a budget

Day 69: The Frog and the Ox

Once upon a time, in a **tranquil** meadow surrounded by swaying wildflowers, a small frog named Freddy lived happily. His daily adventures led him to observe the **massive** ox, Oliver, who grazed nearby. Oliver, the largest and strongest creature in the meadow, commanded respect from all and Freddy greatly **admired** him.

One sunny day, Freddy couldn't help but feel a twinge of envy as he watched Oliver. "If only I were as big as Oliver," he thought. Driven by this desire, Freddy decided to approach Oliver and share his thoughts. **Hopping** over with a cheerful "Hello," Freddy began a conversation with the wise ox.

"Hello, little friend," responded Oliver, lowering his massive head to meet Freddy's gaze. "What brings you here?"

Expressing his longing to be as impressive as Oliver, Freddy shared his feelings. Oliver, with a chuckle, decided to teach Freddy a valuable lesson. He inflated his chest, making himself even larger than usual. However, to everyone's surprise, Oliver's efforts were in vain, and he let out a loud "POP!" The meadow echoed with the sound of escaping air.

Freddy couldn't help but giggle at the sight. "Well, Oliver, it seems that trying to be something you're not doesn't always work."

Oliver nodded, acknowledging Freddy's wisdom. "You're right, Freddy. Embrace who you are and be proud of your unique qualities. Size may impress some, but true greatness comes from being yourself."

From that day forward, Freddy learned to appreciate his small size and the unique details that made him special. The meadow echoed with the laughter of the little frog, who had discovered that being content with oneself was the key to true happiness.

The Moral

The moral of this fable is: "Be happy with who you are and appreciate your own unique qualities. Trying to be someone you're not might not bring the happiness you seek."

Vocabulary

hopping: Jumping.

admired: Looked up to.

mighty: Very large or strong.

massive: Huge.

tranquil: Peaceful and quiet.

Comprehension Questions

1. Why did Freddy, the little frog, approach Oliver, the mighty ox?
2. What did Oliver, the wise ox, do to try to teach Freddy a lesson?
3. What happened when Oliver tried to make himself even larger?
4. What did Freddy learn from the experience with Oliver?
5. What did Freddy realize about true greatness through his encounter with Oliver?

Answers

1. Freddy approached Oliver because he admired the ox's size and strength and wished he could be as impressive.
2. Oliver inflated his chest, making himself even larger than usual, in an attempt to show Freddy the challenges that come with trying to be something you're not.
3. When Oliver inflated his chest, he let out a loud "POP!" as the air escaped, teaching Freddy that trying to be something you're not can have unexpected consequences.
4. Freddy learned to embrace who he was and appreciate his own unique qualities instead of wishing to be someone else.
5. Freddy realized that true greatness comes from being oneself, and it's not necessarily linked to size or outward appearances.

Day 70: Lifestyle Changes

Kim is talking to Tanya about her health.

Kim: Did you **go to the doctor**? I know you were **not feeling well**.

Tanya: I did. She didn't **diagnose me** with anything but said that I'd need to make some serious **lifestyle changes**. My **overall health** is quite poor.

Kim: Oh no! What did she recommend?

Tanya: She said that I have to **reduce my stress**, **get plenty of sleep**, and **eat a balanced diet**.

Kim: That doesn't sound so bad. Do you have to **quit smoking**?

Tanya: Oh yeah, that too. It **shook me up**. She said that if I didn't change, my **life expectancy** would decrease.

Vocabulary

go to the doctor: Have an appointment with a doctor.

not feeling well: Feeling sick.

diagnose me: Assign a name to a health problem.

lifestyle changes: Change in what you eat, how much you exercise and other unhealthy habits like smoking or drinking alcohol.

overall health: General level of healthiness/unhealthiness.

reduce my stress: Decrease the amount of stress in your life.

get plenty of sleep: Sleep eight hours a night.

eat a balanced diet: Eating mostly healthy food from all the food groups.

quit smoking: Stop using cigarettes.

shook me up: Made me feel nervous, worried, or anxious.

life expectancy: How long you can expect to live.

Practice

1. In Canada, the average _____ for men is 84 years.

2. Please _____. It seems like you've been sick for a while now.

3. You'll have to make some _____ to reduce your chance of a heart attack.

4. It _____ when he told me that he wanted to get divorced.

5. I'm _____. I need to go home early today.

6. I hope that I can _____ by changing jobs.

7. My goal is to _____ this year but I know it won't be easy.

8. Please try to _____ if you want to lower your cholesterol.

9. My doctor didn't _____ with anything but just said that I had to stop drinking so much coffee.

10. His _____ is quite good, considering how old he is.

11. Please try to _____ before your exam. You'll be able to think more clearly.

Answers

1. life expectancy

2. go to the doctor

3. lifestyle changes

4. shook me up

5. not feeling well

6. reduce my stress

7. quit smoking

8. eat a balanced diet

9. diagnose me

10. overall health

11. get plenty of sleep

Day 71: An Introduction to Medicine

Medicine, a field as **ancient** as human civilization itself, is a dynamic and ever-evolving discipline that encompasses the study, diagnosis, treatment, and prevention of diseases. Rooted in a rich history of scientific inquiry and guided by ethical principles, medicine plays a pivotal role in safeguarding and enhancing human health. The journey of medicine from ancient healing practices to cutting-edge technologies reflects the **ceaseless** pursuit of understanding the complexities of the human body and the relentless quest for innovative solutions to health challenges.

Historical Foundations: From Ancient Healing to Modern Medicine

The origins of medicine can be traced back to ancient civilizations where healers relied on a blend of empirical observations, folklore, and spiritual beliefs to address **ailments**. Ancient Egyptian, Greek, Indian, and Chinese civilizations made significant contributions to early medical knowledge, laying the groundwork for the systematic study of the human body and its functions. Hippocrates, often regarded as the father of Western medicine, introduced a scientific approach to healing, emphasizing observation and documentation.

The Renaissance marked a revival of scientific inquiry and a renewed interest in anatomy and physiology. Visionaries like Andreas Vesalius challenged age-old beliefs, pioneering dissections to gain a deeper understanding of the human body's structure. This period laid the foundation for the scientific method, setting the stage for the systematic and evidence-based practice of medicine that we recognize today.

The Evolution of Medical Education and Practice

Advancements in medical education and the professionalization of medicine further propelled the field forward. The establishment of medical schools and the formal training of physicians became integral to ensuring a standardized and comprehensive approach to healthcare. The 19th and 20th centuries witnessed **groundbreaking** discoveries, such as the germ theory of disease, vaccination, and the development of antibiotics, revolutionizing the treatment and prevention of infections.

As medicine progressed, specialization emerged, with physicians focusing on **specific** organ systems or disease categories. This specialization allowed for in-depth expertise and improved patient outcomes. Concurrently, interdisciplinary collaboration became a hallmark of modern healthcare, bringing together physicians, nurses, pharmacists, and other healthcare professionals to provide holistic and patient-centered care.

Medical Ethics: The Moral Compass of Healthcare

Embedded within the practice of medicine is a commitment to ethical principles that guide the interactions between healthcare providers and patients. The Hippocratic Oath, a foundational ethical code for physicians, underscores the importance of beneficence, non-maleficence, autonomy, and justice in medical practice. Medical ethics addresses dilemmas arising from technological advancements, cultural diversity, and the balancing of individual and societal interests.

Technological Revolution: Innovations Shaping Modern Medicine

The 21st century has ushered in a technological revolution that is transforming the landscape of medicine. From genomics and precision medicine to artificial intelligence and telemedicine, cutting-edge technologies are enhancing diagnostic accuracy, treatment efficacy, and patient care. Personalized medicine tailors treatments to an individual's unique genetic makeup, offering the potential for more targeted and effective interventions.

Telemedicine has expanded access to healthcare, allowing patients to consult with healthcare professionals remotely. Mobile health applications, wearable devices, and health informatics are empowering individuals to actively engage in managing their health. The integration of big data analytics is revolutionizing medical research, enabling the identification of patterns and trends that can inform public health strategies and medical interventions.

Global Health Challenges: Navigating the Complexities

Medicine is not confined to the realms of individual health but extends to addressing global health challenges. Infectious diseases, non-communicable diseases, and health disparities pose complex issues that require international collaboration and innovative solutions. Public health initiatives, vaccination campaigns, and advocacy for equitable access to healthcare resources are crucial components of the global health agenda.

Conclusion: The Ongoing Quest for Health and Healing

In conclusion, medicine stands at the intersection of scientific discovery, ethical principles, and technological innovation. From ancient healing practices to the frontiers of genomics and artificial intelligence, the field has continually adapted to meet the evolving needs of humanity. As medicine continues its journey into the future, the commitment to advancing health, alleviating suffering, and promoting well-being remains unwavering. The intricate tapestry of medicine weaves together a legacy of healing, discovery, and compassion, embodying the enduring human quest for health and healing.

Vocabulary

medicine: The field of study and practice concerned with the diagnosis, treatment, and prevention of diseases to maintain or restore health.

diagnosis: The process of determining the nature and cause of a medical condition or disease through examination, observation, and testing.

treatment: The application of medical interventions, therapies, or procedures to manage, alleviate, or cure a health condition.

prevention: Measures and actions taken to avoid the occurrence or development of diseases, often through lifestyle changes, vaccinations, and public health initiatives.

ethics: The principles and moral guidelines governing the conduct of healthcare professionals, emphasizing values such as integrity, beneficence, and respect for patients' autonomy.

specialization: The focus on a specific area of medicine or healthcare, allowing practitioners to develop expertise in a particular field, such as cardiology or neurology.

genomics: The study of an organism's complete set of genes (genome), including their structure, function, and interaction, with implications for personalized medicine.

telemedicine: The use of technology, such as video calls and remote monitoring, to provide medical care and consultations at a distance.

precision medicine: An approach to healthcare that customizes medical treatment and interventions based on individual characteristics, including genetic makeup, lifestyle, and environmental factors.

global health: The study and promotion of health and well-being on a global scale, addressing health issues that transcend national borders and require international cooperation.

Vocabulary Challenge

1. Ancient, in the first paragraph is most closely related to:

    a) something very old

    b) showing signs of wear and tear

    c) an old person

    d) something no longer in existence

2. Ceaseless, in the first paragraph is most closely related to:

    a) wait

    b) to stop

    c) continuing

    d) never ending

3. Ailments, in the second paragraph is most closely related to:

   a) related to drinking alcohol

   b) an illness you will die from

   c) an illness

   d) a treatment for an illness

4. Groundbreaking, in the fourth paragraph is most closely related to:

   a) to dig

   b) innovative

   c) gathering information about something

   d) to find something

5. Specific, in the fifth paragraph is most closely related to:

   a) clearly defined

   b) a medical treatment

   c) related to a species

   d) denotes a volume

Answers

   1. a

   2. d

   3. c

   4. b

   5. a

Multiple Choice Questions

1. What is the primary focus of medicine?

   a. Engineering

   b. Diagnosis, treatment, and prevention of diseases

   c. Agriculture

   d. Astronomy

2. What term refers to the process of determining the nature and cause of a medical condition?

   a. Prognosis

   b. Diagnosis

   c. Prescription

   d. Treatment

3. What are measures taken to avoid the occurrence or development of diseases?

   a. Treatment

   b. Intervention

   c. Prevention

   d. Diagnostics

4. Which term describes the principles and moral guidelines governing the conduct of healthcare professionals?

   a. Laws

   b. Regulations

   c. Ethics

   d. Morals

5. What does the term "genomics" refer to in the context of medicine?

    a. Study of the Earth

    b. Study of genes and their functions

    c. Study of infectious diseases

    d. Study of ancient civilizations

6. What is the practice of providing medical care and consultations at a distance using technology called?

    a. Digital healthcare

    b. Telemedicine

    c. Virtual reality medicine

    d. Cybernetic healthcare

7. What is the concept of customizing medical treatment based on individual characteristics, including genetic makeup?

    a. Holistic medicine

    b. Precision medicine

    c. Alternative medicine

    d. Experimental medicine

8. What is the field of study that focuses on a specific area of medicine, allowing practitioners to develop expertise?

    a. General practice

    b. Specialization

    c. Multidisciplinary medicine

    d. Comprehensive care

9. Which term refers to the complete set of genes in an organism, including their structure, function, and interaction?

 a. Genetics

 b. Genome

 c. Genotype

 d. Genitalia

10. What is the study and promotion of health on a global scale, addressing health issues that transcend national borders?

 a. National Health

 b. International Healthcare

 c. Global Health

 d. Public Health

Answers

 1. b

 2. b

 3. c

 4. c

 5. b

 6. b

 7. b

 8. b

 9. b

 10. c

Day 72: You can't Judge a Book by Its Cover

Jerry and Linda are talking about one of their new neighbors.

Jerry: Have you met our new neighbor yet?

Linda: I talked to him last night but he's **a hard nut to crack**. He only gave one-word answers to all my questions!

Jerry: Well, **you can't judge a book by its cover**. I'm sure we'll find out more about him as time goes on. Maybe he's not that **talkative.**

Linda: Maybe. But I felt frustrated talking to him for just a few minutes. Anyway, I'm working on not **burning bridges** so I'll **put my best foot forward**!

Jerry: Good plan. You never know **what may come**. Let's invite him over for dinner and see if he **opens up**.

Vocabulary

you can't judge a book by its cover: to not judge something or someone based on appearance. For example, a restaurant that's not stylish and new may have delicious food.

a hard nut to crack: Someone that is difficult to get to know.

burning bridges: Damaging relationships.

put my best foot forward: To be on one's best behaviour.

what may come: What could happen in the future.

talkative: Someone who likes to talk a lot.

opens up: Shares information about oneself.

Practice

1. I try my best to avoid _____ when leaving a job.

2. I'm happy for the fresh start and want to _____ at this new job.

3. My dad rarely talks and is _____.

4. I learned early on in life that _____.

5. I'm well prepared for _____.

6. My daughter is so _____. I go for a walk every day to get a break!

7. I love it when my son _____ to me. It happens so rarely!

Answers

1. burning bridges

2. put my best foot forward

3. a hard nut to crack

4. you can't judge a book by its cover

5. what may come

6. talkative

7. opens up

Day 73: Applying for University

Cindy is in grade 12, which is an important time for Canadian young people! It's the last year of high school, and students have to decide what they want to do when they **graduate**. There are lots of options! Getting a job, going to a **community college**, learning a **trade**, or university. Cindy got good grades in high school, so she decided to go to university. She eventually wanted to be a teacher, so this was necessary.

There are lots of universities in Canada, so she had to decide which ones to apply to. She lived in a small town in Manitoba, but she wanted to go to a bigger city. Her top two choices were Toronto and Vancouver so she applied to the University of Toronto, Simon Fraser University (in Burnaby, a suburb of Vancouver), and the University of British Columbia (UBC) in Vancouver.

Her first choice was UBC because it had an excellent **education program**, plus Vancouver is an amazing place to live. But, it's also quite difficult to get into UBC because it's **competitive**. You need to get quite high grades in high school to even be considered. After she had sent in her applications, she had to wait for a few months to hear back from the universities.

The first school she heard from was the University of Toronto. She didn't get accepted. She felt disappointed and hoped that she would hear better news from the universities in Vancouver. After a few more weeks, she heard from Simon Fraser. Good news! She got in. And then the next day, she also got good news from UBC.

It was an easy decision. UBC! The other good thing about UBC is that they had a new **student residence** where she could get a private room. It was a beautiful new building and each first-year student could get their own room. This was much better than Simon Fraser University where you had to share a room with a roommate. She replied back to UBC and accepted the offer. She told her friends and family members who were all excited for her. Of course, they would miss her, but they were happy that she got into her first choice.

Vocabulary

graduate: Finish an education program.

community college: Like a university but much smaller. Usually has 1-2 year programs.

trade (job): Trade job examples are a plumber, mechanic, carpenter, etc.

education program: Where people who want to be teachers learn to teach.

competitive: Not easy to win. In this case, not easy to get into a certain university.

student residence: A place where university students live, usually on campus.

Comprehension Questions

1. Why is grade 12 important for Canadians?
2. Do all Canadian students go to university?
3. What is Cindy going to do after high school?
4. Where does Cindy want to go to school?
5. Which schools did she get accepted to?
6. Where is she going to study?

Answers

1. It's important because it's the last year of high school and students have to decide what to do after that.
2. No, there are lots of other options besides university.
3. She's going to go to university.
4. She wants to go to a school in Toronto or Vancouver.
5. She got into Simon Fraser University and UBC.
6. She's going to study at UBC.

Let's Talk More

1. What are common things for people to do in your country after high school? What's the best thing in your opinion?

2. What are some factors that people consider when making this decision?

3. What are some positive and negative things about doing a trade? Would you consider doing a trade?

4. Did you go to university or college? How many places did you apply to?

5. In the future, would you prefer to live in a bigger or a smaller city? Why?

Day 74: Good With Computers

Terry is talking to Sienna about his computer problems.

Terry: Hey, you're **good with computer**s, right? I'm trying to write an essay that's due tomorrow, but my **computer freezes** every couple of minutes. And then . . .

Sienna: Hold on. First things first. Did you **shut down your computer** yet?

Terry: No, should I do that?

Sienna: Yes, and then **restart the computer**.

Terry: Okay, it says it's going to do some **scheduled maintenance** and **install updates**.

Sienna: Let that run and once it starts, do a **virus scan.** It should work a lot better now.

Vocabulary

good with computers: Describes someone who knows how to use computers well.

computer freezes: The computer operating system stops working. For example, you can't click anything on the computer screen

hold on: Wait.

first things first: Do the most important thing first before jumping ahead to other action/things.

shut down your computer: Turn off the computer.

restart the computer: Turn back on the computer after turning it off.

scheduled maintenance: Routine maintenance that helps a computer operating system function well.

install updates: This usually refers to a computer or other electronic device. Involves updating the software.

virus scan: A program that looks for harmful viruses on a computer.

Practice

1. Let's run a _____ first to see if we can catch any problems that way.

2. Just _____ a minute. Did you restart your computer? That's the first thing you should do.

3. Always _____ as soon as possible for your electronic devices to avoid problems.

4. Ted is _____. Let's ask him for some help.

5. _____. Let's get some snacks and drinks for our study session.

6. The network will be down for _____ tonight from 2 am to 4 am.

7. Did you _____ your computer yet? I think that might help.

8. I hate that my _____ at the worst possible times.

9. _____ before going home for the day. I want to save money on electricity.

Answers

1. virus scan

2. hold on

3. install updates

4. good with computers

5. first things first

6. scheduled maintenance

7. restart the computer

8. computer freezes

9. shut down your computer

Day 75: Goofing Around

Andy and Matt are talking about their kids.

Andy: How's it going these days?

Matt: Oh, I'm feeling like I might **snap** at any moment. My kids alternate between **goofing around** and **beating each other up.** I wish they'd **cut it out** and act normally.

Andy: That sounds tough. They'll **grow up** before you know it though! Enjoy it while they're young.

Matt: I know that but they **wear me down**. I hate **dealing with** their battles.

Andy: Lighten up a little! Let them **battle it out**. I know it's bad but I let my kids **get away with** murder! It helps me stay sane.

Vocabulary

snap: Get suddenly angry.

goofing around: Being silly or joking with someone.

beating each other up: Hitting or being physically violent towards each other.

cut it out: Stop doing something.

grow up: Get bigger or older.

wear me down: Make me feel tired and weary.

dealing with: Handling.

lighten up: Relax; not take things so seriously.

battle it out: Fight until there's a winner.

get away with: To do something bad but not receive punishment for it.

Practice

1. I'm not sure you should get in between them. Why not let them _____?

2. My kids _____! I need to take a walk every day to get a break.

3. Hey, stop _____. We need to get some things done.

4. You should _____. It'll be better for your mental health.

5. Kids _____ so quickly.

6. I'm going to _____ if you don't stop that.

7. The pen tapping annoys me. Please _____.

8. I know you're _____ a lot right now. Can I help by watching your kids tonight?

9. Do you think we can _____ it? I'm worried that we won't.

10. My cat and dog love _____.

Answers

1. battle it out

2. wear me down

3. goofing around

4. lighten up

5. grow up

6. snap

7. cut it out

8. dealing with

9. get away with

10. beating each other up

Day 76: Art History

Art history, a captivating exploration of humanity's creative endeavors, **unveils** the visual narratives that span the ages. As a discipline that **delves** into the evolution of artistic expressions across different cultures, periods, and styles, art history provides a lens through which we can comprehend the depth and diversity of human imagination. From ancient cave paintings to contemporary installations, art history invites us to **decipher** the meanings, contexts, and techniques that artists employ to communicate their ideas, emotions, and experiences.

The Dawn of Artistic Expression

The journey through art history begins with the earliest forms of creative expression found in prehistoric cave paintings. Dating back tens of thousands of years, these **primitive** artworks, discovered in locations like Lascaux and Altamira, offer a glimpse into the symbolic and ritualistic aspects of early human societies.

The Flourishing of Ancient Civilizations

As civilizations emerged, so did more sophisticated artistic practices. The art of ancient Egypt, with its monumental sculptures and intricate hieroglyphics, reflected a society deeply **intertwined** with religion and the afterlife. Meanwhile, the classical art of ancient Greece celebrated human anatomy and idealized beauty, influencing generations of artists to come.

The Sacred and the Divine in Medieval Art

During the medieval period, art became a powerful tool for conveying religious narratives and spirituality. Illuminated manuscripts, stained glass windows, and religious paintings adorned churches and monasteries, with artists conveying divine themes through symbolic imagery.

The Renaissance: Rebirth of Humanism and Realism

The Renaissance marked a transformative period in art history, characterized by a revival of classical ideas and a renewed focus on humanism. Artists like Leonardo da Vinci and Michelangelo explored the intricacies of human anatomy, perspective, and emotion, ushering in an era of unprecedented realism and innovation.

Baroque: Theatricality and Emotional Intensity

The Baroque period brought forth a dramatic and dynamic style that aimed to evoke strong emotional responses. Artists such as Caravaggio and Rembrandt used chiaroscuro and tenebrism to create intense contrasts of light and shadow, heightening the emotional impact of their works.

Rococo and the Enlightenment

In contrast, the Rococo period embraced a more ornate and decorative aesthetic, reflecting the values of the Enlightenment. Artists like Jean-Honoré Fragonard captured the elegance and refinement of aristocratic life, while others, like Jacques-Louis David, used art as a means to convey political and moral messages.

Romanticism: Nature, Emotion, and the Sublime

The Romantic era celebrated individual expression, emotion, and a deep connection to nature. Artists like J.M.W. Turner and Caspar David Friedrich conveyed the awe-inspiring power of the natural world, exploring themes of the sublime and the transcendent.

Impressionism and Post-Impressionism: Capturing Moments and Emotions

The late 19th century witnessed the emergence of Impressionism, a movement that sought to capture the fleeting effects of light and color. Artists like Claude Monet and Vincent van Gogh challenged traditional techniques, paving the way for Post-Impressionists to explore personal expression and symbolism.

Cubism, Surrealism, and the Avant-Garde

The early 20th century saw the rise of avant-garde movements such as Cubism and Surrealism. Pablo Picasso and Georges Braque deconstructed form in Cubist works, while Salvador Dalí and René Magritte explored the realms of the subconscious and dreams in Surrealist art.

Contemporary Art: Diversity, Conceptualism, and Global Perspectives

The latter half of the 20th century and beyond witnessed a proliferation of artistic styles and mediums. From the abstract expressionism of Jackson Pollock to the conceptual art of Marcel Duchamp, contemporary art reflects a diversity of voices, perspectives, and forms, challenging traditional boundaries and definitions.

Conclusion: Art History as a Window to Cultural Evolution

In conclusion, art history serves as a captivating journey through the visual tapestry of human creativity. From the symbolic imprints of our prehistoric ancestors to the boundary-breaking expressions of contemporary artists, each period reveals the aspirations, values, and societal shifts that shape artistic endeavors. As we explore the vast spectrum of artistic achievements, we gain not only a deeper understanding of the past but also a profound appreciation for the enduring power of artistic expression in shaping our collective human experience.

Vocabulary

art history: The academic discipline that studies the evolution of visual art forms across cultures, periods, and styles, analyzing their cultural, historical, and aesthetic significance.

prehistoric art: Artistic expressions predating written history, often found in the form of cave paintings, carvings, and artifacts, providing insights into early human societies.

renaissance: A period in European art history (14th to 17th centuries) characterized by a revival of classical influences, humanism, and a renewed emphasis on realistic representation.

baroque: An artistic style prevalent in the 17th century known for its dramatic, emotional intensity, ornate detailing, and grandeur in both visual arts and music.

impressionism: An art movement of the late 19th century that focused on capturing the immediate effects of light and color in the natural world, often characterized by loose brushstrokes.

abstract expressionism: A post-World War II art movement emphasizing spontaneous, non-representational forms of expression, often involving large-scale canvases and gestural brushwork.

surrealism: An avant-garde movement of the 20th century that sought to explore the irrational and subconscious realms of the mind, often creating dreamlike and fantastical imagery.

modern art: A broad term encompassing art produced from the late 19th to mid-20th century, marked by a departure from traditional styles and a focus on innovation and experimentation.

contemporary art: Artistic practices from the mid-20th century onwards, reflecting diverse styles, mediums, and themes, often challenging traditional conventions and embracing new technologies.

avant-garde: An experimental and innovative approach to art that pushes the boundaries of established norms, often associated with pioneering movements and artists challenging the status quo.

Vocabulary Challenge

1. Unveils, in the first paragraph is most closely related to:

   a) removes a face or head covering

   b) part of a public ceremony

   c) covers

   d) shows

2. Delves, in the first paragraph is most closely related to:

   a) researches

   b) excavate

   c) reach inside something

   d) dig

3. Decipher, in the first paragraph is most closely related to:

   a) converting one text to another

   b) interpret something

   c) break a code

   d) move water from one place to another

4. Primitive, in the second paragraph is most closely related to:

   a) pre-Renaissance artist

   b) a basic level of comfort

   c) describes something from ancient times

   d) uncomfortable

5. Intertwined, in the third paragraph is most closely related to:

   a) things twisted together

   b) mixed up

   c) mixed into

   d) connected closely

Answers

   1. d

   2. a

   3. c

   4. c

   5. d

227

Multiple Choice Questions

1. In which historical period did the Renaissance occur?

   a. Ancient Greece

   b. Medieval

   c. Renaissance

   d. Baroque

2. What art movement of the late 19th century focused on capturing the immediate effects of light and color in the natural world?

   a. Baroque

   b. Cubism

   c. Impressionism

   d. Surrealism

3. Which artistic style is characterized by ornate detailing, dramatic intensity, and grandeur, prevalent in the 17th century?

   a. Rococo

   b. Baroque

   c. Renaissance

   d. Neoclassicism

4. What artistic movement emerged in the mid-20th century, emphasizing spontaneous, non-representational forms of expression?

   a. Abstract Expressionism

   b. Cubism

   c. Surrealism

   d. Impressionism

5. Which movement sought to explore the irrational and subconscious realms of the mind, creating dreamlike and fantastical imagery?

a. Cubism

b. Surrealism

c. Impressionism

d. Abstract Expressionism

6. What is the broad term encompassing art produced from the late 19th to mid-20th century, marked by a departure from traditional styles?

a. Renaissance Art

b. Modern Art

c. Baroque Art

d. Impressionist Art

7. Which period preceded the Renaissance and is characterized by art focused on religious themes and symbolism?

a. Ancient Greece

b. Baroque

c. Medieval

d. Rococo

8. What movement challenged traditional conventions and embraced new technologies in art from the mid-20th century onwards?

a. Romanticism

b. Contemporary Art

c. Neoclassicism

d. Abstract Expressionism

9. In which movement did artists like Picasso and Braque deconstruct form and perspective, introducing a fragmented, multi-perspective approach?

a. Surrealism

b. Impressionism

c. Cubism

d. Baroque

10. What term refers to an experimental and innovative approach to art that pushes the boundaries of established norms?

a. Avant-Garde

b. Classicism

c. Renaissance

d. Impressionism

Answers

1. c

2. c

3. b

4. a

5. b

6. b

7. c

8. b

9. c

10. a

Day 77: Ample Time

Ethan is talking to his professor after class about his assignment.

Ethan: Hi, I'd like to follow up about those emails I sent you. I asked if I could get an **extension** on that assignment. But, you didn't email back.

Professor: I didn't email back because I've been very clear. There are no extensions in my classes. You had **ample** time—I told you about the assignment more than a month ago. You can't **deny** that you had enough time if you were organized.

Ethan: Yes, but I have a midterm exam in another class this week too.

Professor: That's the life of a student, isn't it? I know that my policy may seem **harsh** but is your future boss going to be kind if you keep missing deadlines? I've never **misled** anyone about my policy. I've stated it at least 10 times.

Ethan: Who else can I talk to about this? Who is your boss?

Professor: You will not **coerce** me, or my boss into giving you an extension. I recommend that you don't **persist** with this. It will get you nothing. Focus your time and attention on your assignment! You still have one more day. That's an **adequate** amount of time.

Vocabulary

extension: The act of making something longer.

ample: Plentiful; enough.

deny: State that something isn't true.

harsh: Not gentle.

misled: Gave the wrong idea about something.

coerce: Force someone to do something that they don't want to do.

persist: Continuing with something, especially when facing opposition.

adequate: Enough to suit your needs.

Practice

1. Do you think Professor Bolen will give me an _____? My grandmother is in the hospital.

2. The contractors _____ about how much the final cost would be.

3. You have _____ time to finish your homework before soccer practice. If you don't finish, you won't be able to go to soccer.

4. My salary is _____, but not enough for luxuries.

5. Stop trying to _____ me. I'm not going to do it.

6. You can't _____ that I'm better at managing finances.

7. It's a bit _____, but I think we should take away Toni's computer for a week. What she did was so bad.

8. If you _____ in asking me, I'm just going to get angry.

Answers

1. extension

2. misled

3. ample

4. adequate

5. coerce

6. deny

7. harsh

8. persist

Day 78: Breaking Up

Emily had been dating her boyfriend, David, for two years, and they had shared many beautiful moments. However, as time went on, Emily started feeling that something was missing in their relationship.

One sunny afternoon, Emily invited David to meet her at their favorite coffee shop. She sat nervously at a corner table, waiting for him to arrive. When he finally walked in, Emily could tell that something was wrong. David looked distant and **preoccupied.**

They ordered their drinks and sat down. Emily took a deep breath and **mustered up** the courage to speak her mind. "David, I think we need to talk," she said softly.

David looked surprised but nodded. "Sure, Emily. What's on your mind?"

Emily took a moment to collect her thoughts. She knew that what she was about to say would hurt them both, but she also knew it was the right thing to do. "David, I've been feeling like we're **growing apart**. We've changed a lot since we first started dating, and I think it's time for us to break up."

David's face fell, and his eyes filled with sadness. "But Emily, I thought we were happy together. Can't we work things out?"

Emily reached across the table and gently held David's hand. "I understand how you feel, David, but I believe this is the best decision for both of us. We've been drifting apart, and it's not fair to either of us to stay in a relationship that doesn't make us truly happy."

David sighed and nodded reluctantly. "I guess you're right, Emily. It's just hard to let go of what we had."

Tears welled up in Emily's eyes as she spoke, her voice filled with emotion. "I know it's difficult, David. We had some wonderful times together, and I will always cherish those memories. But we both deserve to find happiness and fulfillment in our lives, even if it means letting go of what we had."

They sat in silence for a while, absorbing the weight of their decision. It was **a painful moment** for both of them, but they also knew that sometimes letting go was the only way to grow.

Finally, David broke the silence. "Emily, thank you for being honest with me. I appreciate our time together, and I hope we can still be friends."

Emily managed a small smile through her tears. "I would like that, David. It will take time, but I believe we can remain friends and support each other in our journeys."

As they left the coffee shop, their hands no longer **intertwined**, Emily and David knew that their paths would diverge. The breakup was difficult, but it also marked the beginning of new possibilities and opportunities for both of them.

Months passed, and Emily and David slowly rebuilt their lives. They each found new hobbies, made new friends, and discovered a sense of independence. They often ran into each other in town, exchanging friendly smiles and genuine well-wishes. Emily realized that breaking up with David was the right decision.

Vocabulary

preoccupied: Distracted, thinking of something else.

mustered up: Gathered; brought together.

growing apart: Becoming less close.

a painful moment: A short period of time that is difficult.

intertwined: Connected, or linked closely.

Comprehension Questions

1. Why did Emily want to break up?
2. Did David and Emily used to fight a lot?
3. How did David feel about breaking up?
4. Did Emily find it easy to break up with David?
5. Did David and Emily remain friends afterwards?

Answers

1. She felt like something was missing in their relationship.

2. The story doesn't give up information about this, but it seems like they didn't.

3. He didn't want to break up; he thought they could work it out.

4. No, even though it was her decision, it wasn't easy.

5. They are on friendly terms, but it's unclear if they're friends or not.

Let's Talk More

1. Do you think most breakups go as smoothly as the one in this story?

2. Have you ever gone through a painful breakup?

3. What are some things that people do to feel better about life when they break up with someone?

4. What do you think about ghosting someone, if you've only been dating for a few weeks or a few months?

5. Is there a "nice" way to break up with someone?

Day 79: Hiring Process

Sally and Martin about talking about someone they need to hire at work.

Sally: Hey Marty, we need to talk about Tom leaving. It's a **key role** we have to fill thoughtfully. We have a **tendency to** rush through the **hiring process** but it's such a **demanding job** that I don't think we can do that this time.

Marty: Of course, I agree 100% with you. I'm interested in that guy Jim Jones. Do you remember him? He **did a presentation** at that conference we were at.

Sally: I was **impressed with** him too. He won't just **quit his job** though! We'll have to pay him an extremely **competitive salary** to get him to leave.

Marty: I'll **ask around** and see people in that position are getting paid these days.

Vocabulary

key role: An important position.

tendency to: Usually acts in a certain way.

hiring process: Putting up a job ad, taking applications, doing interviews, etc. From start to finish.

demanding job: A job that is difficult and time-consuming.

did a presentation: Spoke in front of other people about a certain topic.

impressed with: Felt admiration or respect for.

quit his job: Gave notice that he would stop working at his job.

competitive salary: A salary that is similar to what other companies are paying.

ask around: Enquire.

Practice

1. Let me _____. I'm sure someone knows a good plumber.

2. Let's fast-track the _____. We needed someone yesterday.

3. The CFO is a _____ in all organizations.

4. I _____ at the conference last year but I think I'm going to skip this year.

5. A _____ for a good salesperson is more than $100,000.

6. He has a _____ to rush through his homework so he can play video games.

7. I think he should _____. What a terrible boss.

8. It's a _____ but it also comes with a very high salary.

9. I'm _____ how well he did on that test.

Answers

1. ask around

2. hiring process

3. key role

4. did a presentation

5. competitive salary

6. tendency to

7. quit his job

8. demanding job

9. impressed with

Day 80: The Ant and the Grasshopper

In a bustling meadow, there lived two neighbors – an ant named Andy and a **carefree** grasshopper named Greg. They were different from each other in their attitudes towards life.

Andy, the ant, was diligent and hardworking. He spent his days collecting and **storing** food and building a sturdy anthill to prepare for winter. Greg, the grasshopper, loved to hop around, play his cheerful tunes, and enjoy the warm sunshine without a care in the world.

As the days turned cooler, Andy continued to work **tirelessly**, storing food and reinforcing his anthill. Greg, however, continued to sing and dance, believing that the good times would never end.

One day, a chill filled the air, and dark clouds gathered in the sky. Winter was **approaching**. Andy had more than enough food stored to survive the cold months ahead a and he **thrived.** Meanwhile, Greg found himself hungry and **shivering**, realizing he hadn't prepared for the harsh winter.

Desperate and cold, Greg approached Andy's anthill and humbly asked, "Andy, could you spare some food? I didn't plan for winter, and now I'm in need." Andy looked at Greg with a mix of sympathy and disappointment. "I warned you to prepare, Greg. Now, I must focus on my own survival," he replied.

Realizing his mistake, Greg felt a pang of regret. He had spent the warm months playing and not thinking about the future. Now, he had to face the consequences of his actions.

As winter set in, Andy stayed warm and well-fed in his cozy anthill, while Greg struggled in the cold. The once carefree grasshopper learned the importance of planning and hard work the hard way.

The story of Andy, the industrious ant, and Greg, the carefree grasshopper, teaches us that preparation and hard work lead to success, while negligence can result in hardship. It's a valuable lesson about the importance of planning for the future.

The Moral

The moral of the story is: "It's important to work hard and plan for the future so that you can be prepared for tough times."

Vocabulary

storing: Keeping for future use.

carefree: Without worry.

thrived: Did well.

approached: Got nearer.

shivering: Shaking a little bit due to cold.

Comprehension Questions

1. Who were the two friends in the story?
2. What did Andy do to prepare for winter?
3. How did Greg spend his time while Andy was preparing for winter?
4. When winter arrived, how did Andy and Greg do?
5. What is the moral of the story?

Answers

1. The two friends in the story were Andy, the hardworking ant, and Greg, the playful grasshopper.
2. Andy worked hard, storing food for winter, and reinforcing his anthill.
3. Greg spent his time playing, not making preparations for winter.
4. Andy thrived in winter because he had stored enough food and made preparations. Greg struggled because he hadn't planned for the cold season.
5. The moral of the story is that it's important to work hard and plan for the future.

Day 81: The Goose that Laid the Golden Eggs

Once upon a time in a quaint village, there was a poor farmer named Jack and his wife, Emma. They owned a small farm with a few animals, including a goose. One day, to their surprise, the goose laid a **golden** egg. The couple was overjoyed and couldn't believe their luck.

The news spread quickly, and soon, the whole village learned about the magical goose. Every morning, the goose would lay a single golden egg. Jack and Emma became the talk of the town, and people from far and wide came to witness the extraordinary event.

As time went by, Jack and Emma's life changed. They became more and more **wealthy** with each golden egg, and their once simple farmhouse transformed into a grand **mansion**. The couple was living a comfortable life, thanks to the magical goose.

However, as their wealth grew, so did their **greed**. Jack couldn't help but wonder if there were more golden eggs inside the goose. One day, unable to resist his **curiosity**, he decided to cut the goose open, thinking he could get all the golden eggs at once. To his dismay, the goose had no more golden eggs inside. Jack's hasty decision had cost him the source of his fortune. The couple was left with regret and an ordinary goose.

The moral of the story is that greed can lead to loss. Jack and Emma had a good life with the golden eggs, but their desire for more made them lose everything. It teaches us to be content with what we have and not to let greed cloud our judgment.

And so, the once-magical goose continued to live on the farm, reminding everyone in the village about the consequences of greed. Jack and Emma learned a valuable lesson, and the village returned to its peaceful ways, realizing that true wealth comes from appreciating the blessings we already have.

The Moral

The lesson of the story is: Be happy with what you have and don't be too greedy, or you might lose what's important. With wealth sometimes come **peril.**

Vocabulary

golden: Made of gold.

wealthy: Very rich.

greed: Have a selfish desire for something.

mansion: A very large house.

perils: Serious dangers.

Comprehension Questions

1. What did the special goose do every morning?

2. How did Jack and Emma's life change with the golden eggs?

3. Why did Jack cut open the goose?

4. What happened when Jack cut open the goose?

5. What is the moral of the story?

Answers

1. The special goose laid a golden egg every morning.

2. Jack and Emma became wealthy, and their simple farmhouse turned into a grand mansion.

3. Jack was curious and greedy, thinking there might be more golden eggs inside the goose.

4. To Jack's dismay, there were no more golden eggs, and he lost the magical source of wealth.

5. The moral of the story is to be content with what you have and not let greed lead to losing what's important.

Day 82: At a Standstill

Aaron is talking to a librarian on the phone about a book he was trying to find.

Aaron: Hey, this is Aaron Smith. I'm wondering if you've found that book yet.

Librarian: Well, things are **at a standstill for the time being**. I searched **at length** in all the libraries in Canada and had no luck.

Aaron: Is it available in stores?

Librarian: More bad news. It's been **out of print** for more than 20 years, which means that it's **out of stock** everywhere. Sorry to **contradict** what I initially told you, but I did some research and just found this out.

Aaron: Oh no!

Librarian: Your best chance of finding it might be to illegally download it if you can find it. I don't generally recommend it, but it might be your only hope. You may also have to **adjust** your expectations. It will be difficult to find.

Vocabulary

at a standstill: Stopped.

for the time being: At this current time.

at length: For a long time.

out of print: More copies are not being made (usually refers to a book).

out of stock: Not available in stores.

contradict: Give an opposite opinion.

adjust: Change something to make it better.

Practice

1. _____, I'm happy enough with Amy. We do have some problems though.

2. Sorry, that size is _____. How about another color?

3. We talked _____ but couldn't come to an agreement.

4. Talks between the two parties are _____.

5. Why don't we _____ that bike side? You'll have a more comfortable ride.

6. Why do you always _____ everything I say during meetings? I'm so tired of it.

7. That book is _____ now. You'll have a difficult time finding it.

Answers

1. for the time being

2. out of stock

3. at length

4. at a standstill

5. adjust

6. contradict

7. out of print

Day 83: Thanksgiving Dinner

Kim's favorite holiday is Thanksgiving. She loves the food, getting together with family and the changing colours of the leaves. In Canada, Thanksgiving is in October, instead of November like in the USA.

When she was a kid, Kim's grandmother used to cook a big feast that included turkey, ham, **stuffing**, mashed potatoes, sweet potatoes, salads, and pumpkin pie with whipped cream. The adults would have wine, and the kids would have pop. She would eat until she was **stuffed** and then eat a little bit more after that! But her favourite thing was playing with all of her cousins. She'd usually only see them at Thanksgiving, Christmas, and Easter—the biggest holidays in Canada.

When Kim got older, she still enjoyed Thanksgiving with friends and family. Sometimes she'd cook the turkey. It was a big responsibility! You had to take it out of the fridge to **thaw** for a few days. Then, you had to cook it for hours, making sure it was cooked in the middle but not burnt on the outside. There are lots of different ways to season the turkey and everyone has a secret recipe. It isn't easy but everyone said that Kim did a great job with it!

During Covid, Thanksgiving looked a little bit different. Her family members all cooked their own meals at home. The usual things—mashed potatoes with gravy, stuffing, and veggies. Except most people cooked a small chicken instead of turkey. Turkeys are big and are best for at least 10 people. Then, everyone ate together while on a Zoom call. It was a little bit different but still nice to see everyone. They **chatted** for hours and only said goodbye when it started to get late and everyone wanted to clean up all the food and do the dishes. Kim was starting to get sleepy from drinking lots of wine too!

Whether in person or on *Zoom*, one of Kim's favourite **traditions** was for everyone to say what they're thankful for that year. This year, everyone was thankful to be healthy and safe. Others were thankful to have a job and a nice place to live.

Vocabulary

stuffing: Bread with spices, vegetables, butter, etc. that is cooked inside of a turkey.

stuffed: Very full.

thaw: Become not frozen.

chatted: Talked.

traditions: Things that you do every year, usually to celebrate a holiday.

Comprehension Questions

1. Are Canadian and American Thanksgivings on the same day?
2. What are some foods that people eat at Thanksgiving?
3. Why was Thanksgiving different this year?
4. How much does Kim usually eat at Thanksgiving?
5. Is Kim good at cooking turkey?
6. What is one of Kim's favourite Thanksgiving traditions?

Answers

1. No, they aren't. Canadian Thanksgiving is in October while American Thanksgiving is in November.
2. People eat turkey and gravy, mashed potatoes, ham, stuffing, vegetables, sweet potatoes, and pumpkin pie.
3. It was different because of Covid.
4. She eats a lot until she's stuffed.
5. Yes, she's good at it.
6. One of her favorite traditions is saying what everyone is thankful for.

Let's Talk More

1. What's your favorite holiday? Why? How do you celebrate?

2. Have you ever been to a Canadian or American Thanksgiving celebration? How was it?

3. Have you celebrated holidays differently because of Covid-19? How?

4. What are some things that you're thankful for?

5. Does your country have a kind of Thanksgiving/harvest/fall celebration? What is it?

Day 84: On Time

Jill is getting into trouble with her boss Andrea for being late to work.

Andrea: I've noticed that you haven't been **on time** for work most days this past month.

By the time you arrive, everyone is already well underway with their work. It's disruptive.

Jill: **In my defense**, I'm **at loose ends** these days. My mom is sick, and I have two young kids. My husband and I are also getting divorced.

Andrea: Well, **at any rate**, we expect everyone to be here by 9:00 most days of the week.

On balance, the work you do is excellent, so we don't want to let you go. You can use your holidays if you have to for sick kids or parents or whatever.

Jill: Okay. I didn't realize it was so serious. I'll figure it out.

Andrea: Okay.

Vocabulary

on time: Arriving before, or at the specified time.

by the time: Describes something that has already happened when another thing occurs.

in my defense: In support of.

at loose ends: Disorganized, struggling, not knowing what to do.

at any rate: Used to emphasize the following statement.

on balance: In summary; in general.

Practice

1. My son is _____ unless I manage his homework. I hate it.

2. _____, you'll need to get it done by the weekend.

3. _____, I did look after Tommy a lot over spring break.

4. _____ Jen arrived for the party, I was getting ready to leave.

5. In my view, _____ is 5-10 minutes early!

Answers

1. at loose ends

2. at any rate

3. in my defense

4. by the time

5. on time

Day 85: The Crow and the Pitcher

Once upon a time, in a sunny meadow bordered by tall trees, there lived a clever crow named Charlie. One scorching summer day, the heat was **unbearable**, and Charlie found himself desperately thirsty. His usual **streams** had dried up, and he began searching for a refreshing drink.

After a relentless search, Charlie finally spotted a **pitcher** partially buried in the ground. Excitement filled him as he hurried towards it, hoping to find some water. However, to his dismay, the water level in the pitcher was too low for him to reach with his beak.

Undeterred, Charlie pondered for a moment. Then, his eyes gleamed with an idea. He looked around and noticed a collection of shiny **pebbles scattered** nearby. With determination, Charlie picked up the pebbles, one by one, and dropped them into the pitcher.

As each pebble fell into the pitcher, the water level gradually rose. Charlie continued this clever strategy, patiently adding more pebbles until the water reached a level where he could finally take a refreshing drink.

His thirst was **quenched**, and Charlie thanked his creativity and problem-solving skills. With a triumphant caw, he flew away, leaving behind a valuable lesson for anyone who witnessed his ingenuity.

The story of Charlie and the pitcher teaches us that intelligence, creativity, and perseverance can help overcome challenges. Instead of giving up when faced with difficulties, like Charlie, we can find innovative solutions by thinking smartly and utilizing the resources around us.

The Moral

The moral of the story is: "Being clever and using your creativity can help you find solutions to problems, even when things seem difficult."

Vocabulary

pitcher: A container used for holding liquids.

pebbles: Small rocks.

streams: Small rivers.

quenched: Satisfied thirst by drinking something.

unbearable: Not able to be endured or tolerated.

scattered: Found in a random fashion, not all together.

Comprehension Questions

1. Why was Charlie the crow thirsty?

2. What did Charlie find when he was thirsty?

3. Why couldn't Charlie reach the water in the pitcher?

4. What did Charlie use to solve the problem and reach the water?

5. What is the moral of the story?

Answers

1. Charlie was thirsty because it was a very hot day, and he couldn't find any water.

2. Charlie found a pitcher with a little water inside.

3. The water in the pitcher was too low for Charlie to reach with his beak.

4. Charlie used shiny pebbles. He dropped them into the pitcher one by one to make the water level rise.

5. The moral of the story is that being clever and using creativity can help find solutions to problems, even when things seem difficult.

Day 86: Turn Over

Police officers are talking about how to get a criminal to turn someone in.

Police officer #1: I think we should **turn up** the heat on this guy. I'm sure he'll **turn over** his accomplice. Or, at least help up **track him down**.

Police officer #2: I think you're right. He's already told us enough to **narrow down** the search. I was just about to **punch out** but I'll **stick around** for a bit.

Police officer #1: Okay, do you want to question him this time? I'll **back off** for now. But, don't **let up** too much.

Vocabulary

turn up: Increase.

turn over: Give something up.

track him down: Find him.

narrow down: Eliminate some possible options.

punch out: Finish work for the day.

stick around: Stay.

back off: Draw back.

let up: Reduce or lessen whatever you're doing.

Practice

1. Don't _____ on him, okay? He's just starting to brush his teeth without us telling him every single time.

2. Let's _____ the oven. I want it to cook quickly. I'm so hungry.

3. I know you want to _____ but there are still a couple more things to do.

4. Let's _____ so we can find out why he's missed so much school.

5. Please _____. I know you're trying to help but I don't want to hear it anymore.

6. I'm hoping to _____ the choices online first so we don't waste so much time in the store.

7. We have to _____ the keys next Friday.

8. Let's _____ until the end and see if there's any leftover alcohol we can take home.

Answers

1. let up

2. turn up

3. punch out

4. track him down

5. back off

6. narrow down

7. turn over

8. stick around

Day 87: When Pigs Fly

Jerry and Linda are talking about their kids.

Jerry: My kids are **buttering me up** because they don't want to have to help put up **Christmas lights.**

Linda: You're lucky that you can get some help **once in a while**. My kids never **pitch in** for stuff like that. **When pigs fly**, right?

Jerry: Ah, it's all **smoke and mirrors** at my house usually. My kids **make a show out of** cleaning up after themselves after dinner but their rooms are still like a **pigsty**.

Linda: What have we gotten ourselves into?

Vocabulary

when pigs fly: Something that is very unlikely to happen.

pitch in: To contribute to or help with something.

buttering me up: To flatter or please someone because you want something in return. For example, a child who is extra nice to their parents around Christmas because they want an expensive video game system.

smoke and mirrors: Flashy things that distract from what is real.

Christmas lights: Lights on houses for decoration around Christmas.

once in a while: Sometimes.

make a show out of: To do something in a flashy way.

pigsty: Usually refers to a very messy room or space.

Practice

1. I like to let loose _____.

2. His presentation was all _____. No real substance.

3. My kids love to help me put up _____.

4. We all _____ every Saturday morning to clean up the house.

5. My kid's bedroom is a _____.

6. My mom always used to say, "_____" when I asked her for money!

7. I know when my kids are _____ but I fall for it anyway. Their sweet smiles!

8. I hate that my coworkers always _____ finishing even the smallest task.

Answers

1. once in a while

2. smoke and mirrors

3. Christmas lights

4. pitch in

5. pigsty

6. When pigs fly

7. buttering me up

8. make a show out of

Day 88: Fall Down

Sam and Tommy are talking about the old shed in their yard.

Sam: Hey, you know that old shed out back that's about to **fall down**? I think we should **clear it out** and make space for a volleyball court back there.

Tommy: Should we **burn it down** or **knock it over**?

Sam: I'd **go along with** either but I do like the idea of **lighting it up**. We could **kick back** with a beer and watch!

Tommy: Will it burn well do you think?

Sam: I'm not sure. Maybe we could **chop up** the wood a bit first and **find out**.

Vocabulary

fall down: A tree, shed, house, person, etc. collapses.

clear it out: Remove.

burn it down: Burn something until there's nothing left.

knock over: Make something fall by using force.

go along with: Agree with.

lighting it up: Burning it.

kick back: Relax.

chop up: Use an axe or knife to make something smaller (wood, vegetables, etc.)

find out: Discover; see the results.

Practice

1. Let's _____ what time your soccer game is.

2. That room? Let's _____ and make space for a home office.

3. Please _____ these veggies and put them in the soup.

4. I want them to _____ that old house. It's such an eyesore.

5. Let's _____ with a beer. I'm so tired.

6. Let me know when you're _____. I'd like to see it.

7. That cake looks kind of unstable. Is it going to _____?

8. This house! I wish we could just _____. It's so messy.

9. I'm happy to _____ with whatever. I'm flexible.

Answers

1. find out

2. clear it out

3. chop up

4. knock over

5. kick back

6. lighting it up

7. fall down

8. burn it down

9. go along with

Day 89: The New Italian Restaurant

Reading strategy focus: *Look at the words in **bold**. If you don't know the meaning, make a guess based on the other words in the sentence. Do not use a dictionary. Then, read the questions below and the story.*

Sam and Tony were out for a walk in their neighborhood when they noticed a big line up. "I wonder why they're lining up? Hmmm. It looks like a new restaurant," said Tony. They asked someone in the line what they were waiting for. The person said that it's a new Italian restaurant, Luigi's. They had become popular because of a **review** in **the Vancouver Sun**. The person reviewing the restaurant loved it and said that it was now the best Italian in Vancouver. This made everyone want to try it as well!

Sam and Tony decided to **check it out** on Friday night. Tony called to make a reservation but Luigi's said that they don't take reservations. They would just have to line up and hopefully get a seat. Sam guessed that it wouldn't be that busy if they went earlier so they decided to go at 5:00.

Friday night came and they walked over to Luigi's. They got there at 5:00 and there was already a line up of about 20 people. They decided to wait. It would probably be worth it. Sam and Tony chatted with people while they waited. Everyone was excited to try the food. Some people were going to try the pasta while others wanted pizza. Luigi's used a brick oven for making pizza, just like in Italy.

Finally, after about an hour, they got a table. Sam ordered a glass of white wine while Tony went with red. The waiter also brought them some bread and oil and balsamic vinegar to dip it in. They ordered two things to share: spaghetti & meatballs and a **margherita pizza**. They liked to try a bit of everything so usually ordered things to share. The food came quickly which surprised them because the restaurant was **packed.**

It was the best Italian food either of them had ever tried. Although it was expensive, it was worth it. For dessert, they had homemade **tiramisu** and some Italian coffee. When the meal was done, they paid the bill and left a generous **tip**. Sam said, "Tomorrow night? Same time, same place?" He was joking but Tony said, "YES! I want to try everything."

Vocabulary

review: An opinion about something. In this case, about Luigi's restaurant.

the Vancouver Sun: A newspaper in Vancouver.

check it out: Go to, look at, examine, etc. In this case, go to the restaurant.

margherita pizza: Pizza with tomato sauce, basil and mozzarella cheese.

packed: Filled with people; completely full.

tiramisu: An Italian dessert.

tip: Money someone gives for good service at a restaurant, hotel, hair shop, etc.

Comprehension Questions

1. Why is Luigi's so busy?
2. Does the restaurant take reservations?
3. When did they decide to go there?
4. Why did Sam and Tony go there at 5:00?
5. What did they order?
6. Did they like the food?

Answers

1. It's because of a good review in the *Vancouver Sun*.
2. They don't take reservations.
3. They decided to go on Friday for dinner.
4. They thought it wouldn't be so busy at 5:00 (instead of later).
5. They ordered wine, pizza, pasta, tiramisu and coffee.
6. They loved it. They want to go back soon!

Synonym Practice: Think of two other words or phrases that have the same meaning as the vocabulary words from the story. Do NOT look at the definitions again, if possible.

1. check out: _____, _____
2. packed: _____, _____
3. review: _____, _____

258

Summarize the Story

Using 1-2 sentences, summarize the story. Include only the main details and key events.

Summary:

New Words

Write down any new words that you learned from this story. Consider writing them in a vocabulary notebook or making some flashcards for further review.

-

-

-

Let's Talk More

Talk with a friend or classmate about these questions. If you're studying alone, write down 2-3 sentences for each question. There is no correct answer—give your opinion!

1. Have you ever waited in a long line at a restaurant? Was it worth it?
2. What's the best meal you've ever had at a restaurant? Was it a very expensive place?
3. Do you like Italian food? Why or why not?
4. What's your favourite kind of food to eat in a restaurant? Why?

Day 90: Noise Pollution

Kathleen and Kenny are talking about living in Busan.

Kathleen: Kenny! You lived in Busan, South Korea? I've always wanted to go there. What's it like? I've heard that it's a beautiful **coastal city**.

Kenny: Well, there's a lot of **noise pollution** and **light pollution**. It's the second biggest city in Korea. And **traffic jams** too during **rush hour**.

Kathleen: It sounds terrible.

Kenny: Oh no, it's amazing! I love Nampo-Dong, which has lots of **street food** and **street vendors** plus **trendy cafes**. It's perfect for a date.

Kathleen: What else?

Kenny: Well, there's no real **downtown core** or **main square** but there are six beaches within **city limits**. Most people just hang out there, especially in the summertime.

Vocabulary

coastal city: A city next to the ocean.

noise pollution: Ambient noise in a city. For example, cars honking.

light pollution: Light from signs and cars that you can see inside your house at night.

traffic jams: Lots of cars on the road which makes progress slower than normal.

rush hour: The busiest times to drive, usually because of people going to work and coming home from work.

street food: Food from an outside stall.

street vendors: People selling things at an outside stall.

trendy cafes: Coffee shops that are fashionable and hip.

downtown core: The area in a city with lots of tall buildings; an important place of business.

main square: The most important public courtyard in a city.

city limits: The entire city, including suburbs. Not just the downtown core.

Practice

1. I love to buy Christmas presents from _____. There are lots of interesting things.

2. Vancouver is the best _____ in Canada.

3. Within the _____, you can find three beaches and countless parks.

4. Go after 9:30 am to avoid ____.

5. Where's the _____? I'd love to spend some time there and people watch.

6. The best _____ in Korea? Honestly, I can't choose. There are many delicious things.

7. The _____ in Edmonton is famous for being boring at night.

8. ____ makes it difficult for me to sleep at night even though I have blackout curtains.

9. My boyfriend loves to spend time at _____ on weekends. I think they're expensive!

10. During ____, it takes twice as long to get home.

11. The _____ is terrible here. I have to wear earplugs to sleep at night.

Answers

1. street vendors
2. coastal city
3. city limits
4. traffic jams
5. main square
6. street food
7. downtown core
8. light pollution
9. trendy cafes
10. rush hour
11. noise pollution

Day 91: Sit Down

Kendra wants Ethan to help her with a problem with a co-worker.

Kendra: Hey, **come in** and **sit down**. What's up?

Ethan: I'm hoping to **sort out** that issue Ted and I had.

Kendra: Sorry to **cut in**. But, please **hold off** on telling me more. I've heard enough. I've already told you guys to **stay out** of each others' business.

Ethan: Okay, but he keeps **putting me down**.

Kendra: Stop. I'm tired of you two **telling on** each other. Just **stay away** from each other and we'll try to arrange for you to be put on separate sides of the office.

Vocabulary

come in: Enter

sit down: Have a seat in a chair or on a couch.

sort out: Come to an understanding about something.

cut in: Stop someone from talking before they were finished.

hold off: Wait.

stay out: Not go somewhere.

putting me down: Insulting.

telling on: Tattling; complaining about something someone did.

stay away: Not get near.

Practice

1. Please _____ from your brother. He's grumpy right now.

2. Can I _____ before you say more? I already know this information.

3. Please _____ of my office until I invite you in.

4. Can I _____? I'd like to talk to you about something.

5. She's always _____ her brother and it's starting to get very annoying.

6. Please _____ on working overtime on this project. We don't have the budget to pay for it.

7. Would you like to _____?

8. My boss keeps _____ in subtle ways. I don't know how long I can stay at that place.

9. I'm hoping that we can _____ this conflict we're having.

Answers

1. stay away

2. cut in

3. stay out

4. come in

5. telling on

6. hold off

7. sit down

8. putting me down

9. sort out

Day 92: The Blind Date

Reading strategy focus: *Scan the story quickly (set a timer for 30 seconds). Answer this question: Will Sandy and Lucy go on another date? (yes/no). See answer below the story. Then, read the questions and read the story again, more slowly.*

Sandy recently **broke up** with her girlfriend and was feeling sad. They had been together for five years. She was talking to her friends about it over coffee at Starbucks. One of her friends, Sarah said, "Sandy! I know the perfect person for you. She is recently **single** too."

Sarah's friends laughed. She was happily married and always trying to set people up. She was **famous for it.** However, she was often successful so her friends let her do it. Some people she had set up had even gotten married. Sandy said, "Who is it?"

Sarah told everyone about one of her co-workers, Lucy. She had just moved to Toronto recently and started working at Sarah's company. Sarah said that she was beautiful, athletic and nice as well. Sandy was **uncertain**. She still felt sad about her previous girlfriend. But her friends said that she had nothing to lose and should meet Lucy. Sandy **reluctantly** agreed and Sarah said that she'd talk to Lucy on Monday at work and see what she thought. Sandy felt nervous, even thinking about it.

On Monday afternoon, Sandy got a text from Sarah. Lucy agreed to meet her and would send a text tonight after work. After work, Sandy got a text message from Lucy that said, "Hi! I'm Lucy. Nice to meet you. I've heard a lot about you. Would you like to meet up this week for a walk?" Sandy agreed and they made a plan to meet on Wednesday. Sandy felt nervous but also excited. Lucy seemed amazing, according to Sarah.

On Wednesday, they met at a local park. Lucy was beautiful and engaging, just like Sarah promised. Sandy had a great time and it was easy to talk to Lucy. After the date, Sandy went home and then sent Lucy a text. She said, "It was nice to meet you. Would you like to meet up this weekend?" Lucy replied, "It was nice to meet you, too. But, **you're not my type.** Maybe we could be friends." It wasn't the answer that Sandy expected.

Reading strategy focus answer: No.

Vocabulary

blind date: Going on a date with someone that you've never met in real life.

broke up: Ended a romantic relationship (marriage, or boyfriend/girlfriend).

single: No husband/wife/boyfriend/girlfriend.

famous for it: Known for doing something a lot.

uncertain: Not sure.

reluctantly: With hesitation.

you're not my type: You're not the kind of person I usually like in a romantic way.

Comprehension Questions

1. Why is Sandy feeling sad?
2. What is Sarah famous for?
3. Is Sarah married?
4. When and where did Sandy and Lucy meet?
5. What did Sandy think about Lucy?
6. What did Lucy think about Sandy?

Answers

1. Sandy ended her relationship a little while ago and is feeling depressed about it.
2. She is famous for setting up her single friends.
3. Yes, she is happily married.
4. They met on Wednesday at a park.
5. She thought Lucy was beautiful and engaging.
6. Lucy thought that Sandy wasn't her type.

Synonym Practice: Think of two other words or phrases that have the same meaning as the vocabulary words from the story. Do NOT look at the definitions again, if possible.

1. broke up: _____, _____

2. uncertain: _____, _____

3. reluctantly: _____, _____

Summarize the Story

Using 1-2 sentences, summarize the story. Include only the main details and key events.

Summary:

New Words

Write down any new words that you learned from this story. Consider writing them in a vocabulary notebook or making some flashcards for further review.

-

-

-

Let's Talk More

1. Have you ever been on a blind date? How did it go?

2. Have you ever set someone up on a date? How did it go?

3. What's the best way to meet a boyfriend or girlfriend where you live?

4. What are some of the positive and negative things about being single?

Day 93: The Ice Cream Shop

Mandy and Todd are deciding what kind of ice cream to get.

Mandy: There are so many choices here! I'm **like a kid in a candy shop**.

Todd: They don't call it 99 **scoops** for nothing! **What's your fancy?**

Mandy: I know it's boring but I usually **go for** the same thing every time. I get **a double**: cookies & cream and rainbow sherbet.

Todd: Those are **classics** for sure! Can't go wrong with them. **Sticking with** what you love. Not a bad strategy at all.

Mandy: What do you like?

Todd: I like to **mix it up** and get something different every time. I think I'll go for the salted caramel. I'm sure I'll have some **FOMO** when I see the ones you got though!

Vocabulary

like a kid in a candy shop: Feeling very happy! Lots of good things to choose from.

scoops: Refers to ice cream balls.

what's your fancy?: A kind of old-fashioned way to ask, "What do you like/want?"

a double: 2 scoops of ice cream.

classics: The usual things. Not new and trendy.

sticking with: Not choosing something new; going with the familiar.

mix it up: Change something; choose a new thing.

FOMO: Fear of missing out.

Practice

1. All these new cars? I'm _____.

2. Why don't we _____ and get Chinese tonight?

3. I prefer _____ to new releases.

4. Just come. You know you'll have some serious _____ if you don't!

5. How many _____ are you going to get?

6. What do you think about _____ this contractor for next year?

7. _____. I'm thinking of going with pepperoni and mushroom.

8. I'd like _____ please: chocolate and French vanilla.

Answers

1. like a kid in a candy shop

2. mix it up

3. classics

4. FOMO

5. scoops

6. sticking with

7. What's your fancy?

8. a double

Day 94: Sit Tight

Jason and Linda are talking about when to leave to get the train.

Jason: Hey, let's get moving! **Time is money.**

Linda: Sit tight. I need to grab a few things before we go.

Jason: Come on. We have to get to the train station on time. I hate always being the **bad guy** about stuff like this.

Linda: Well, to be fair, you've been as **clear as mud** about what time we needed to leave. Traffic won't be as bad as you think.

Jason: There are always **traffic jams** at this time. Let's **get a move on.**

Linda: Okay, I'll be ready **in the blink of an eye**. Stop bugging me!

Vocabulary

sit tight: Wait patiently and don't take any action right now.

clear as mud: Confusing or not easy to understand.

time is money: To try to get someone to work faster or more efficiently.

traffic jams: When cars aren't moving quickly because it's busy.

get a move on: Hurry up.

bad guy: Someone who always has bad news/enforces a rule.

in the blink of an eye: In a short amount of time.

Practice

1. If you leave after 8 am, there will be lots of _____.

2. Let's _____. I don't want to be late for school.

3. I try to always remember that _____.

4. I had a terrible teacher in high school. His explanations were as _____.

5. _____ while I check and see what time the movie starts.

6. I hate to be the _____ but you need to get it together or you're going to get fired.

7. Don't miss the eclipse. It'll happen _____.

Answers

1. traffic jams

2. get a move on

3. time is money

4. clear as mud

5. Sit tight

6. bad guy

7. in the blink of an eye

Day 95: Down to Earth

Casey is talking to Dan about his crush on Tina.

Dan: Hey, so what's up with you and Tina?

Casey: Seriously, nothing. I have **a crush** on her but I'm too nervous to ask her out. Every time I talk to her, I can never bring myself to do it.

Dan: Stop being such a **chicken**. She's **down to Earth**. She won't be mean if the answer is no.

Casey: I'm just scared of rejection I guess.

Dan: Well, **it's not rocket science**! Just talk to her and see what the **vibe** is. I'm **rooting for you**.

Casey: Give it **another shot**! I'll buy you lunch if you do, no matter what the answer is!

Vocabulary

crush: Initial liking of someone in a romantic way.

chicken: Describes someone who is scared of something.

down to Earth: Easy-going.

it's not rocket science: It's not that difficult to do.

vibe: Feeling.

rooting for you: Cheering for you.

another shot: One more try.

Practice

1. Just give it _____. I'm sure you'll get it.

2. Don't be such a _____ and just do it!

3. Honestly, _____. I have no idea what's taking him so long.

4. We're all _____.

5. She's very _____ and easy to talk to.

6. Did you hear that Ted has a _____ on Sally?

7. What's the _____ like?

Answers

1. another shot

2. chicken

3. it's not rocket science

4. rooting for you

5. down to Earth

6. crush

7. vibe

Day 96: Holding Up

Andy is annoyed at Nicole for not cleaning the sink.

Andy: Hey Nicole. The drain is **clogged up** again with your long hairs. You're not **holding up** your end of the bargain. Remember? You promised to clean the sink and I promised to **knock off** the late-night video gaming.

Nicole: Oh, **come off it**. It's not a big deal. I could **do with** you not hassling me all the time.

Andy: You **went back on** your word! I **carried out** my end of the deal. You **let me down**.

Nicole: Okay, you're right. I **messed up** and I'm sorry. I'll pay more attention to it.

Vocabulary

clogged up: Blocked.

holding up: Doing something you promised.

knock off: Stop.

come off it: Stop saying something silly or ridiculous.

do with: Get something you want.

went back on: Didn't follow through; broke a promise.

carried out: Did something as promised.

let me down: Disappointed me.

messed up: Did something incorrectly.

Practice

1. Sorry. I _____ on that project. I'll do my best to fix it.

2. He _____ his word—I was so disappointed in him.

3. He's famous for not _____ his end of the deal. Such a sketchy guy.

4. I have a feeling he's going to _____ in the end but so far, so good.

5. I could _____ a cup of tea.

6. The drain is _____ again. Could you please take a look at it?

7. He _____ each task efficiently and under budget.

8. Oh, _____. That's not what happened.

9. Please _____ all the swearing around Jamie, okay? I don't want her to hear that stuff at home.

Answers

1. messed up

2. went back on

3. holding up

4. let me down

5. do with

6. clogged up

7. carried out

8. come off it

9. knock off

Day 97: Watching Hockey

Reading strategy focus: *Scan the story quickly (set a timer for 30 seconds). Answer this question: Is Lucy happy or sad about the outcome of the game? See answer below the story. Then, read the questions and read the story again, more slowly.*

Lucy had loved watching hockey for as long as she could remember. She grew up in Edmonton during the 1980's and watched some of the most famous players there: Wayne Gretzky, Paul Coffee, Yari Kurri, Mark Messier, and others. One of her favourite memories was watching Edmonton win the **Stanley Cup** many times when she was young. Her dad used to take her to the games when she was little.

Hockey is probably the most popular sport in Canada. It makes sense. Canada is a big place with cold winters and lots of snow and ice! Many boys and girls play hockey when they're kids. Some of them will even play in the Olympics or the **NHL**. People that like hockey usually have a favourite team that they cheer for. The Toronto Maple Leafs and the Vancouver Canucks are the most popular teams in Canada. However, Edmonton now has the best player in the world, Connor McDavid so they're becoming more popular.

Lucy now lives in Calgary but her favourite team is still the Edmonton Oilers. The Calgary Flames and Edmonton Oilers are in the same province, Alberta. When they play each other, it's called, "The Battle of Alberta." The teams and the fans don't like each other very much and there are often fights among players.

The Oilers were coming to play in Calgary so Lucy and her friend (also a fan of the Oilers) got tickets. They wore their Oilers **jerseys** and hats to the game and **cheered** loudly whenever the Oilers made a good play or got a goal. Everyone around them was angry and annoyed at them for cheering for Edmonton, instead of Calgary. But Lucy and her friend just laughed and cheered louder. There were only a few Edmonton fans in the whole arena.

There are three, 20-minute periods in a hockey game. The Flames were leading 2-0 after the end of the first period. The two teams played the second period and it was still 2-0. In the third period, the Oilers scored two goals in the first few minutes. The game was

tied. When there was only 3 minutes left, the Oiler's captain, Connor McDavid scored a beautiful **goal**. In the end, the Oilers won the game 3-2. Lucy and her friend cheered until they had no voice left. It was a fantastic game and even better because the Oilers came out on top.

Reading strategy focus answer: She's happy.

Vocabulary

Stanley Cup: The trophy that the best team in the NHL gets.

NHL: National Hockey League. The highest professional hockey league in Canada and the USA.

jerseys: What sports players wear (or fans).

cheered: Yelled and clapped hands to support a person or team.

tied: The same score (1-1, or 3-3 for example).

goal: Getting a hockey puck in the net. Or, ball in soccer. Used in many other sports too.

Comprehension Questions

1. What is Lucy's favourite hockey team?
2. Why does she like this team?
3. Where does Lucy live now?
4. What is it called when the Calgary Flames and the Edmonton Oilers play each other?
5. How long is a hockey game?
6. Who won the game?

Answers

1. Her favourite hockey team is the Edmonton Oilers.

2. She likes them because she grew up in Edmonton.

3. She lives in Calgary.

4. It's called the Battle of Alberta.

5. It's 60 minutes (3, 20-minute periods).

6. Edmonton won the game.

Synonym Practice: Think of two other words or phrases that have the same meaning as the vocabulary words from the story. Do NOT look at the definitions again, if possible.

1. jersey: _____, _____

2. goal: _____, _____

3. cheer: _____, _____

Summarize the Story

Using 1-2 sentences, summarize the story. Include only the main details and key events.
Summary:

New Words

Write down any new words that you learned from this story. Consider writing them in a vocabulary notebook or making some flashcards for further review.

-

-

-

Let's Talk More

1. Have you ever seen an ice hockey game? What did you think about it? If not, what's your favorite sport to watch?

2. Are you a fan of any sports team? Do you have a jersey?

3. In your country, what are some of the most popular sports to play and watch?

4. What are some sports that you know of where people can make physical contact with each other? (like hockey)

Day 98: Swag

Angela and Lucy are talking about a gig tonight.

Angela: Hey, did I hear that you're playing a **gig** tonight at the Metro?

Lucy: Yeah, do you want to come?

Angela: Are you giving away any **swag**?

Lucy: No **freebies**! It's such a myth that musicians make **megabucks**. Most of us are **struggling to make ends meet**.

Angela: Okay, okay! I'll come anyways. What time?

Lucy: 10:45.

Angela: So late. But I'll **catch some Z's** now so I'll be good for later. **Break a leg**!

Vocabulary

gig: A concert or performance, somewhat informal.

swag: Something free you get at an event.

freebies: Something free, in any situation.

megabucks: Lots of money.

struggling to make ends meet: Finding it difficult to make enough money to pay all the bills.

catch some Z's: Get some sleep.

break a leg: An expression to say, "Good luck" to someone just about to go on stage.

Practice

1. Hey, _____ tonight, okay?

2. They don't pay her the _____ for nothing!

3. Did you get some good _____ at the conference?

4. _____ and we'll talk later.

5. Let's go to Costco on Saturday afternoon. They always have so many _____.

6. Can you come to my _____ this weekend?

7. Sid is _____. Should we try to help him out?

Answers

1. break a leg

2. megabucks

3. swag

4. catch some Z's

5. freebies

6. gig

7. struggling to make ends meet

Day 99: Trade In

Kari is talking to Jen about getting a new car.

Kari: Hi, I'd like to **trade in** this car if possible and upgrade to a better one.

Jen: I'm sure we could **work something out**. Can I **point out** some of the options for new cars?

Kari: Hang on. You can maybe **talk me into** a new car but I have to **stick to** my budget pretty strictly so it would have to be a cheaper one.

Jen: Sure, let's have a **look around**. Why don't you **think about** a Kia? I could **go down** a bit on price if your old car is in reasonable shape.

Vocabulary

trade in: Exchange something old, usually for a newer thing.

work something out: Make a deal.

point out: Highlight or feature.

hang on: Wait.

talk me into: Convince.

stick to: Not cheat (a diet), not exceed (a budget), etc.

look around: Check out the items or a location.

think about: Consider.

go down: Reduce.

Practice

1. Can you come back in a few minutes? I'd like to have a _____ first.

2. I'd like to _____ all the features.

3. Are you able to _____ on price at all? It's just above my budget.

4. It's so hard to _____ my diet around Christmas.

5. Can you please give me some time to _____ that? I'm not sure where I'll be next year.

6. I think you could _____ getting that game console for the kids.

7. I'm sure we could _____ to compensate you for all this extra time that you're working.

8. _____ a second. I'd like to take a closer look at the contract before I sign in.

9. I'd like to _____ this phone for a newer one, please.

Answers

1. look around

2. point out

3. go down

4. stick to

5. think about

6. talk me into

7. work something out

8. hang on

9. trade in

Day 100 Coming Down With Something

Jimmy's dad is checking to see if he's sick.

Dad: Hey Jimmy, you don't look great. Are you **coming down with** something? Let me feel your forehead.

Jimmy: Dad! I feel fine.

Dad: You're **burning up**. We'll have to **call off** that birthday party of yours tomorrow. **Go back** to bed. And **stay off** electronics for the entire day. And don't **monkey around with** your new puppy. You need rest.

Jimmy: Dad, no! I'm okay. I don't want to **lie around** all day. And I for sure want to have my party tomorrow.

Dad: I told you this would happen if you kept **staying up** late playing video games. You're **run down**.

Vocabulary

coming down with: Getting sick.

burning up: Having a fever.

call off: Cancel.

go back: Return to somewhere you previously were.

stay off: Not use.

monkey around with: Play with; fool around.

lie around: Be lazy in bed or on the couch.

staying up: Not going to bed, usually late at night.

run down: Not in the best of health due to working too much, staying up late, etc.

Practice

1. I'm starting to get _____. Something has to give.

2. Why don't you _____ to school? You could get a much better job.

3. Hey, you're _____. I'll make a doctor's appointment for you.

4. Why are you _____ so late? You look exhausted.

5. Please _____ electronics in the mornings. I just got a call from your principal that you're always late for school.

6. I hope I'm not _____ that cold that my son had.

7. I love to _____ on rainy weekends.

8. My kids love to _____ with the neighbor kids after school.

9. Let's _____ that meeting. I think we've already solved the issue.

Answers

1. run down

2. go back

3. burning up

4. staying up

5. stay off

6. coming down with

7. lie around

8. monkey around with

9. call off

Before You Go

If you found this book useful, please leave a review wherever you bought it. You might also be interested in these other resources (by Jackie Bolen). You can find them wherever you like to buy books:

- Advanced English Conversation Dialogues

- The Big Book of Phrasal Verbs in Use

- 100 Days to Better English Speaking (for Intermediate)

Made in United States
Orlando, FL
01 December 2024

54726656R00157